Discovering Nonfiction

25 Powerful Teaching Strategies
Grades 2–6

Harvey F. Silver
Richard W. Strong
Matthew Perini

A Publication of Canter & Associates

Research Assistants
Mary Fran Daley
Gregory Tuculescu
Silver, Strong & Associates

Editorial Staff
Amy Morrell
Carol Provisor
Barbara Schadlow
Kathy Winberry

Design
Barbara Smiley
BJ Nemeth

© 2000 Canter & Associates, Inc.
P.O. Box 66926, Los Angeles, CA 90066-6926
800/262-4347   310/578-4700
www.canter.net

Printed in the United States of America
First printing January 2000
03 02   5 4 3 2

ISBN 1-57271-030-6

PD4182

*To all the teachers who taught us
and to all the teachers
who let us believe we were teaching them.*

Contents

Introduction

The Challenges of Nonfiction Reading

Take a minute and step back from the fury and adventure of life in your classroom. Take a look at your students. Try to imagine their futures—as readers.

> Stefanie loves to argue—perhaps she'll be a lawyer, reading legal briefs. Jared is a real nature lover—always a frog in his pocket or a wounded bird under his arm—maybe he'll be a veterinarian—a good one too, with piles of veterinary journals on the nightstand next to his bed. Sarah and Larry have been making eyes at each other for three months now. Imagine them married, cruising the Internet looking for a good buy on their first home. And Zachary. Chances are he might already be researching stock options or 401k's. Then there's Zoe—the latent politician, the do-gooder. Just try to imagine her not surfing a dozen online newspapers, talking back to the editorials under her breath.

No matter how we picture our students' futures, it is nearly impossible not to see a world in which most of them will spend a good deal more time reading nonfiction than literature. But we do not need to look so far into our students' futures to see that this is true. Their lives in high school and college will be dominated by nonfiction reading: primary documents in history, lab directions in science, French and Spanish newspapers in foreign language class, word problems in mathematics, magazine articles and editorials on nutrition in health, and, of course, all the textbooks.

The point is *not* that students don't read a wide variety of nonfiction texts in elementary school. The point is that most reading instruction in elementary schools concentrates on stories and poems, not on magazine articles, biographies, scientific essays, textbooks, reviews, editorials, or historical diaries.

This is no accident. Children come to school with a rich background as story lovers and story tellers. They may have read stories on their own or had stories read to them, but even if neither of these experiences has been available for them, they have listened to others spin tales in their houses and apartments, watched stories on television and in the movies, and even spun a few tales themselves—if only in response to questions like, "Why didn't you come when I called you?" Some researchers actually believe that the structure of stories is hard-wired into our minds and constitutes a fundamentally human form of cognition (Bruner, 1986). According to this research, we don't have to learn what a story is because the structure of stories is waiting in our neurons as a part of our evolutionary inheritance.

In teaching students to read and understand stories, thoughtful reading teachers follow well-known paths and rely on well-known principles of reading. They:

- **Analyze the special challenges posed by a story's vocabulary and structure** and make these a target of instruction.
- **Activate prior knowledge** by helping students connect what they already know and feel to the events in the story.
- **Address comprehension skills through modeling and guided practice** by using story grammar and higher-order-thinking questions to help students remember and make inferences about literature.
- **Arrange instruction around common story genres,** thus helping students to perceive the differences between fables, fairy tales, myths, and poems.

Unfortunately, nonfiction reading differs significantly from literary reading, and the lessons students learn while reading, discussing, and writing about stories will *not* transfer to nonfiction reading. Though the same principles of good instruction apply to both kinds of reading, the application of these principles to nonfiction texts requires significant changes if students are to become as adept at reading nonfiction as they are at reading stories, poems, and plays.

How Nonfiction Reading Differs From Literary Reading

Nonfiction Texts Do Not Follow the Same Structures as Literature

Nonfiction texts are organized differently than literary texts. Whereas nearly all stories can be understood under a common story grammar (see diagram), nonfiction texts differ significantly in their organization. Some nonfiction texts tell readers the steps they need to follow to achieve a goal (building a bird house, cooking a batch of chocolate chip cookies). Others explain why something happens (causes of the Civil War, where earthquakes come from). Still others attempt to make an argument, explore a decision, or compare two concepts. Most students come to school with a much more limited knowledge of these basic nonfiction structures than they do of the common story structures found in literature.

Characters _____

_____

Setting _____

_____

Problem _____

_____

Resolution _____

_____

| *Traditional story grammar*

Literary Texts Draw on Different Kinds of Background Knowledge than Nonfiction Texts

Stories and poems lie close to our common experience as human beings. They are designed to draw on and activate memories of our experiences to help us see ourselves differently or to entertain and surprise us with new perspectives. It is only when the people or situations in a story differ markedly from our own that reading and connecting to prior experience becomes difficult.

Nonfiction texts, on the other hand, are designed to tell us what we don't know. Therefore, connecting experiences to prior knowledge is almost always more of a problem in nonfiction texts than it is in fictional ones. What is more, textbook authors in particular are pressured to cover vast amounts of material in little space. Frequently, textbooks make unwarranted assumptions about the background knowledge of their readers by leaving out critical background knowledge necessary for students to understand their texts (Beck, McKeown, Hamilton, & Kucan, 1997). The novelty of the information and the gaps in background knowledge pose special challenges for students when reading nonfiction texts.

Nonfiction Texts Are Designed to Be Remembered and Used

No one is especially concerned if a fourth-grader fails to remember a particular story in *Frog and Toad Are Friends*. As long as she knows how to read, understand, and discuss stories of increasing complexity, no one worries if she doesn't recall the content of a story she read last year. But if a fourth-grader doesn't know the parts of a plant, or that the United States of America is divided into states, or that the blood is pumped through our bodies by the heart while information is stored in the brain, there is reason for concern. This difference in the use of the content of nonfiction texts means that it is far more important for students to know how to remember and retell the gist of nonfiction texts than it is for them to perform these acts for fictional texts. And, whereas a single incident or detail can make a story or poem meaningful to a student, nonfiction texts most often require students to separate important from unimportant information in terms of the text, and not merely in terms of their own interests and patterns of finding relevance.

The Solutions for Nonfiction Reading

Given both the similarities and differences between literary and nonfiction reading, thoughtful teachers of nonfiction reading need to teach according to three principles:

1. Teachers need to spend at least as much time reading and studying nonfiction with their students as they do reading fiction.
2. Both literacy and nonfiction reading need to be based on:
   - Careful modeling of comprehension skills.
   - Guided practice in application of these skills in units organized thematically or by genres.
   - Lots of discussion centered on strategies for overcoming the difficulties in making sense of all kinds of texts.
   - Opportunities for reading-based writing to help students learn how to apply what they are learning about the reading process and their growing content knowledge.
3. Nonfiction reading instruction needs to focus on the skills and strategies best adapted to make sense of nonfiction texts.

With these principles in mind, this book has been designed to help teachers learn and apply the principles of proficient reading and the proficient teaching of reading so that their students become more adept and thoughtful readers of nonfiction.

This book is divided into five chapters, one for each of five skills students need to develop in order to read nonfiction at a high level of proficiency.

CHAPTER ONE contains instructional strategies teachers can use to help students separate essential from nonessential information.

CHAPTER TWO covers notemaking tools students can be taught so they can create meaningful and usable records of their reading.

CHAPTER THREE deals with using strategies to teach students how to deepen their reading by connecting what they know to nonfiction texts, by applying reasoning skills, and by constructing images while reading.

CHAPTER FOUR's purpose is to help students learn how to use questioning strategies to clarify and concentrate their reading.

CHAPTER FIVE explores the connections between reading, writing, and thinking and contains strategies and assessment opportunities for helping students use writing as a tool for enriching, extending, and refining their reading.

Chapter One

What's the Big Idea?

Chapter Overview: Advance Organizer

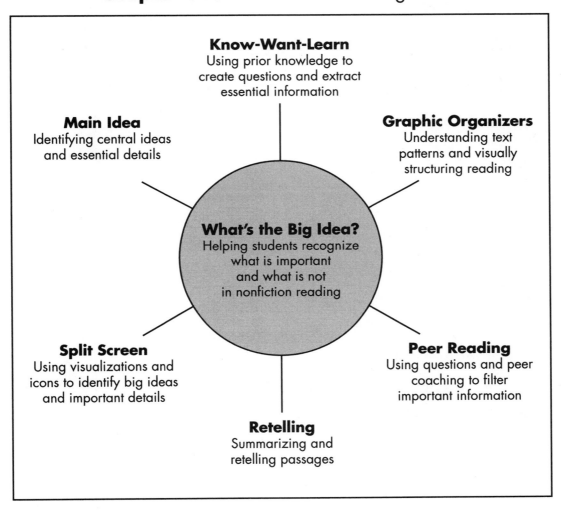

Know-Want-Learn
Using prior knowledge to create questions and extract essential information

Main Idea
Identifying central ideas and essential details

Graphic Organizers
Understanding text patterns and visually structuring reading

What's the Big Idea?
Helping students recognize what is important and what is not in nonfiction reading

Split Screen
Using visualizations and icons to identify big ideas and important details

Peer Reading
Using questions and peer coaching to filter important information

Retelling
Summarizing and retelling passages

> *"How does a main idea become a main idea?"*
>
> Estelle Theander
> Seventh Grade
> Social Studies Teacher

Imagine you were an idea. Not a great idea. Not an important idea. Something smaller and off to the side. Something other people saw as a detail. You lived in a writer's head, or in a reader's mind, or on a page somewhere in a library. But you were ambitious: you wanted to become something more, something bigger, say a main idea. What would you do?

Strange question. But it is a question that lies close to the heart of helping students become thoughtful readers. And, as a question, it is not alone. It resides with a number of equally provocative questions. Questions like:

- Do readers find important ideas, or do they make them up?
- How do authors let you know they think an idea is important?
- How can you tell a main idea from a detail?
- Can an idea be important for one person, but secondary for another?
- What if a nonfiction reading has no main idea?

These questions may seem bothersome and overly philosophical. But the readers in your classroom struggle with them every day. And their struggles become your struggles because, as teachers, we want more than anything for our readers to be successful. We all know that separating the important from the unimportant is an essential reading skill. But how do we know what's important and what's not in the first place?

An Experiment

On the next page are four pieces of nonfiction reading at various levels of complexity. We would like to ask you to read them and identify the important ideas. "What do we mean by important ideas?" you might ask. We mean the key points you find there: what you would tell others about the passage who had not read it so that they got the gist of its content.

Warning: Our point is *not* that an important idea can be whatever you want it to be. Our point is rather to encourage you to look closely at how you determine what is most important in these passages and to ask yourself how this might apply to how you teach your students.

Reading Selection #1

Definition of a Point

A *point* is the basic unit of geometry. It has no size. It is infinitely small. It has only one location. A physical model of a point would be a pencil tip.

Picture of a Point   P •

You can use a dot to represent a point. You name a point with a capital letter. This point is called point P.

Reading Selection #2

Why Were Roads Important to the Roman Empire?

At the height of Roman rule, Roman roads reached to the farthest corners of the empire. This vast network made travel much easier and was directly responsible for the great wealth the Empire gained through trade.

Roman roads were built using three layers of firmly packed rocks that were then covered with slabs of smoother stones. The Romans made great efforts to keep their roads flat, but if a hill or mountain had to be crossed, the Romans preferred a short steep climb to the long trudge around a mountain or hill. By keeping roads flat, Roman troops were able to respond more quickly to rebellions or invasions on their borders. Trade and communication were able to move more rapidly and satisfy the needs of the vast Empire.

Reading Selection #3

Both frogs and toads are tailless amphibians with long hind legs for leaping. But they are not exactly the same. Toads spend more time on land than frogs. While frogs have smooth, slippery skin, toads' skins are rougher and dryer. And toads tend to have broader bodies than frogs.

Reading Selection #4

The circulatory system circulates blood throughout the body using the heart and three kinds of blood vessels—arteries, capillaries, and veins. The most important part of the circulatory system is the *heart*. The heart is a very strong muscle that pumps blood into the arteries when it contracts and takes blood in from the veins when it relaxes. *Blood* is a liquid that delivers oxygen to all the body's parts and carries away chemical waste for disposal. Blood travels away from the heart through the arteries and then crosses through the *capillaries* into the veins. The veins carry the blood back to the heart, where it will soon be recycled and used again.

Reading selections in which to identify the main ideas

What the Research Says

So how did you do? How did you determine what was important in each passage? Two recent books on reading provide insight into what proficient and thoughtful readers do as they try to determine what is and is not important in the nonfiction texts they read. Both Keene and Zimmermann's *Mosaic of Thought* (1997) and Marzano and Paynter's *New Approaches to Literacy* (1994) paint very similar pictures of what proficient readers do as they try to identify the important information in what they read. Proficient readers, whether seven or seventy, do four things as they read nonfiction prose. As you read these four behaviors, keep track of how you read the sample passages. Did you exhibit any of these behaviors in your reading?

Proficient Readers of Nonfiction . . .

✔ Use a sense of purpose and especially questions to screen the information in what they read. In this way, they separate information relevant to the question from information that is not. Thus, questions and purposes act like a spotlight, focusing the mind's attention on what is truly important. (Selection two, for instance, sets up a purpose for reading by providing you with a pre-reading question.)

✔ Pay attention to patterns in nonfiction writings by asking: Is this passage comparing and contrasting, is it describing a process, laying out a sequence of events, explaining causes and effects? (You may have noticed this in your own reading of selection three, which follows a compare and contrast pattern.)

✔ Use the clues authors provide, such as highlighted topics and subtopics, illustrations, phrases like "most important," and stated and unstated main ideas. (What you may have done with selection one or selection four.)

✔ Retell and summarize passages as they read or through rereading. Proficient readers do a lot of rereading in order to check and monitor their understanding. (What you probably did anytime a passage became difficult.)

How thoughtful readers of nonfiction extract important information

What This Means for Teaching Nonfiction Reading

Most of the skills described here are performed more or less unconsciously by proficient readers. In order to create students who are successful at identifying what is important in nonfiction texts, we need to teach students:

- How to use the questions we give them and how to create questions of their own to guide their reading.
- How to recognize the most common textual patterns for nonfiction and how to use these patterns to identify what is and is not important.
- How to use clues an author provides to identify main ideas and supportive details.
- How to successfully summarize and retell the important information both during and after reading.

In the remainder of this chapter, we will provide you with five research-based strategies derived from the above four principles.

The Main Idea helps students identify the central or main ideas and the relevant details that support it.

Graphic Organizers help students understand text patterns and use visual constructions to structure their reading.

Know-Want-Learn helps students activate prior knowledge to create questions as a guide for an information search.

Peer Reading helps students use questions to filter out the most important information in what they read.

Retelling helps students summarize and retell passages.

Split Screen helps students use icons and visual representations to identify big ideas and important details.

THE MAIN IDEA

The Strategy in Action

Marcia Bars is conducting a lesson on finding main ideas with her second graders, who are reading *Reptiles Do the Strangest Things,* by Leonora and Arthur Hornblow (1970). She begins by saying to her students, "Sometimes when I read I become a little confused about what I'm reading. Does that ever happen to you?"

"Yes," many of her students say.

"That's happening to me right now. All these different reptiles have made me a little confused. When this happens, I ask myself, 'Who or what is the focus of what I'm reading?' In this case, everything in this passage seems to be about . . ."

"The hog-nose snake."

"Right," Marcia says and writes *hog-nose snake* at the top of the shoebox organizer (see diagram) she has prepared on the blackboard. (Marcia already has discussed with her students how a paragraph is like a shoebox: because details are stored or contained inside it.) "Next, I ask myself: What is the passage telling me about hog-nose snakes? Now I see that the reading is about the hog-nose snakes and it seems to be saying that hog-nose snakes do strange things to protect themselves from being eaten by enemies." Marcia writes *do strange things to protect themselves* on the shoebox. "Finally, I check my idea by looking to see if the details in what I'm reading support my idea that hog-nose snakes do strange things to protect themselves. Do you see any clues that these snakes do weird or funny things when they are threatened?"

"They puff up their bodies."

"They lash their tails and hiss."

"They don't have venom or a rattle so they have to do other things."

"They hiss."

"They play dead."

"They lie upside down."

As students volunteer their ideas, Marcia records them on the shoebox.

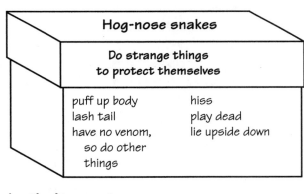

Shoebox organizer

When the class has completed filling in the organizer, Marcia reviews the three questions she used to help her find the main idea:

1. Who or what is the focus of this reading?
2. What is the passage telling me about this topic?
3. What words or clues in the passage support my idea?

Later on during reading time, students practice looking for main ideas using Marcia's three questions as they read their own books.

Why the Strategy Is Beneficial

Perhaps no element in reading instruction is as confused and muddled as our concept of Main Idea. In their research on how main ideas are conceived in school, Moore, Cunningham, and Rudisill (1983) found that when teachers ask students for a main idea, they may be asking them to:

- Give the *gist* of what they have read.
- Provide an *interpretation*.
- Supply a *key word*.
- Create a *title*.
- Name a *topic*.
- Identify an *issue*.
- Write a *summary*.
- Describe a *theme*.
- Analyze a text and discover a *thesis*.

This confusion is exacerbated by several factors:

- **The absence of a clear developmental curriculum for helping students identify main ideas.** Most schools stop direct instruction in main idea somewhere between the third or fourth grade—exactly at the point that expository texts become more prevalent and the application of main idea strategies more essential.
- **The lack of clear modeling for main idea identification in passages longer than one or two paragraphs.** Usually, and perhaps in deference to standardized tests and SATs, students are asked to identify main ideas only in short, "closed" passages rather than within larger textual structures.
- **The prevalence of inferred (as opposed to directly stated) main ideas in student texts.** For instance, as Baumann and Serra (1984) have discovered, only 44 percent of the paragraphs in student social studies texts contain a clearly stated main idea and, of those, only 27 percent use this statement as the opening sentence of the paragraph.

The Main Idea strategy helps overcome these difficulties by:

- Modeling the clear difference between:
  a. Finding the topic (the subject of the reading).
  b. Identifying the main idea (a sentence that summarizes the central thought of the reading).
- Showing students how to check findings by assembling and organizing details that support the main idea.

- Providing regular and extended practice in identifying topics, main ideas, and details on progressively longer and more complex passages. This progression should move through collaborative work to independent practice.
- Direct teaching and practice of notemaking using a system that ensures students gradually develop the ability to record notes that are accurate, well organized, and easy to understand (see Chapter Two, "From Notetaking to Notemaking," for a variety of techniques).

How to Use the Strategy

Use Organizer 1-A, "What's the Main Idea?" on page 15.

Incorporate the Main Idea strategy into your classroom using the following steps:

1. Explain to students that there is a difference between the *topic* of a reading and *the main idea:* The *topic* is the subject of the reading. The *main idea* is a sentence that summarizes the central thought the reading provides about the passage.
2. Model the clear differences between the two ideas through teacher Think-Alouds (describing aloud while modeling your internal thinking processes).
3. Explain to students that when the main idea is not specifically stated, they can look for these cues (adapted from Van Dijk and Kintsch, 1983):
   - Print cues—the use of italics, bold-faced type, and subheadings to indicate important topics.
   - Word cues—the use of words like *important, key,* or *significant* as indicators of the most vital information.
   - Sentence cues—the use of summarizing or previewing sentences (or paragraphs) to highlight the information central to the text.
   - Organization cues—the use of standard expository prose structures (sequence, cause and effect, conceptual, descriptive comparison) to provide a pattern to guide student understanding. (See the section on Graphic Organizers, pages 16 to 26.)
4. Show students how to check their identification of the main idea by identifying and organizing details that support it.
5. Select a reading and, using Organizer 1-A, "What's the Main Idea?" guide students through the process of identifying the three elements central to the main idea (topic, main idea, supporting details of the main idea).
6. Provide regular and extended practice in identifying the three elements on progressively longer and more involved readings.
7. Over time, move students through collaborative group work toward independent practice in which students use the strategy as they read on their own.

Helping the Struggling Reader

Struggling readers may need more time and practice illustrating main ideas and details through drawing, sketches, and concept maps (see Information Search, pages 79 to 84, Split Screen, pages 47 to 50, and Concept Mapping, pages 67 to 69).

Also, struggling learners may have difficulty determining main ideas and relevant details because of gaps in their application of grammatical information to reading. For example, below are two sources of confusion struggling readers often experience when looking for main ideas and relevant details (adapted from Burns, Roe, & Ross, 1998):

- **Pronoun Referents**
  "Though many colonists were eager for a conclusive conflict with England, others felt *their* loyalty to *their* mother country came first." (*Their* refers back to others.)
- **Adverb Referents**
  Since reptiles rely more on the sun than mammals do, they will frequently, during cooler periods, find an area free of enemies, fix themselves to a warm rock and remain *there* until the temperature rises. (*There* refers back to the rock)

Trouble with sentences like these is in no sense the fault of students. Striving to create a classroom in which reading instruction and grammatical concepts are closely linked is the best means of addressing the problem.

For students who have not yet grasped the structure of main-idea paragraphs, a tactile model like a shoebox often helps students solidify their understanding. You might start with the main idea "You can find many things at the seashore" by writing it on the box. Then, have students guess some of the items you have placed inside. As you take items out of the box (sand, shells, coins, etc.), explain how they support the main idea. Or, you can reverse the process by taking items out of the box one by one and asking students to construct a main-idea sentence that supports the contents.

Name: _____

What's the Main Idea?

Topic (subject of reading)

Main Idea (sentence that summarizes the central thought)

Details (facts and ideas that support the main idea)

Reflection How I identified the topic and the main idea:

___ It was stated in the reading.

___ I used a cue. ☐ Print cue (italics, bold-face type, subheads) ☐ Word cue ("important," "key," "significant") ☐ Sentence cue
(summarizing or previewing sentence) ☐ Organization cue (sequence, cause and effect, conceptual, descriptive comparison)

GRAPHIC ORGANIZERS

The Strategy in Action

Gary Tucker is conducting a unit on the Civil War with his fifth graders. "Part of understanding history," Gary explains, "is to understand the personalities and beliefs of the people who helped make it. I want you to focus your attention on two people who were in power during the war: Abraham Lincoln and Jefferson Davis. The next two chapters in our book tell us about the personal history and personalities of these two presidents. As you read about Abraham Lincoln and Jefferson Davis, I want you to focus on how these men were similar and how they were different."

Gary then reminds students how to use a compare and contrast organizer to record and organize the important ideas in their reading. During reading time, Gary moves around to help struggling students and to make sure students understand how to use the organizer to gather the appropriate information. Afterward, he reviews the key points on the board with students. Once the organizer is complete (see diagram), Gary asks his students to write a brief essay explaining how each president was uniquely qualified for his job.

Differences — Lincoln	Differences — Davis
Against slavery, especially westward expansion	Pro-slavery, owned slaves
Became famous during debates with Stephen Douglas	Became famous as a hero in war with Mexico
Wanted North and South to remain unified	Argued for Southern power, slavery, and right of states to secede
Calm, logical, never mean-spirited	Mischievous boy. Became serious and studious after malaria
1860—became president of the United States	1861—became president of Confederacy

Similarities

Both born in Kentucky

Both became presidents

Smart

Ambitious

Qualified for their jobs

Compare and contrast organizer

* * *

Joy St. Maarten is teaching an art class. She has asked her students to select an artist of their choice from the books in her library and to prepare a brief oral report on their artist. Specifically, Joy wants her students to focus on a single essential question: "How has the artist's personal biography affected his or her work as an artist?"

To help students prepare, Joy decides to model the process by using a sequence organizer to record major events from the life of artist Georgia O'Keefe. Using an overhead projection of a selection from Robyn Montana Turner's biography of O'Keefe from the *Portraits of Women Artists for Young Children* series, Joy explains, "What I do when reading an artist's biography is select the five most important events from the artist's life. To help me determine if an event is significant, I ask myself: Does the author explain how or why this event affected the artist's life and work? Look, for instance, at the bottom of page seven, where it says that when Georgia was twelve years old, she began taking private drawing and painting lessons. Does it say why this is important to Georgia as an adult?"

"It says Georgia discovered she like to paint," one student says.

"She began painting her own imaginary scenes," says another.

A third student says, "It made her realize she wanted to become an artist."

"Great," Joy says. "It looks like we have a very important event that affected her as an artist. Art lessons made Georgia realize she wanted to be an artist in the first place." Joy records this information in the first section of the sequence organizer.

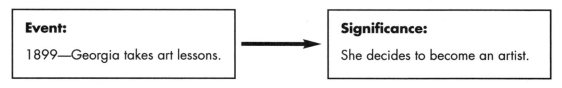

Sequence organizer

Joy continues this modeling process with her students until she has completed the sequence organizer. Students then use this process to conduct research on their chosen artists for their oral presentation.

Why the Strategy Is Beneficial

Often, nonfiction texts are organized according to text patterns that are unfamiliar to young readers. For example, a text explaining the difference between frogs and toads might use a structure of comparison (e.g., "Unlike the toad, the frog has teeth in its mouth"), while a reading on how to serve a tennis ball might follow a pattern of sequence (e.g., "First, you should place your feet approximately two feet apart while standing behind and perpendicular to the baseline"). Readings such as these, or longer readings that contain a variety of text patterns, make it difficult to use a main-idea structure to find the important information. Different reading strategies are needed to extract the relevant information from these types of texts. But when it comes to reading informational texts, especially those that lack clear main ideas, what is it exactly that the proficient reader sees?

Research conducted over the past twenty-five years has consistently provided one answer to this question. What the learner sees is text structure. Many studies, including those conducted by Pearson and Comperell (1994), Ruta (1992), Derewianka (1990), and Jones, Pierce, and Hunter (1989) all verify this conclusion. Text structure refers to the patterns authors use to organize their expository material. Research into text structure regularly notes the following patterns as prominent in the nonfiction readings assigned to students.

Topic Description	Sequence/Cycle	Comparison	Problem/Solution
Provides information organized around central concepts and subtopics.	Places events into a chronological sequence or a series of steps.	Explores the similarities and differences between related events, people, concepts, or ideas.	Lays out a problem or issue and explores one or more solutions and their effects.

Text-structure patterns in nonfiction readings

Proficient readers have, through extensive reading, learned to use clues in the text to determine the text pattern and then used the pattern to help them anticipate what kinds of information the text is likely to provide and what particular aspects of that information are likely to be important.

On the other hand, average and struggling readers frequently are unable to structure what they are learning or to determine what is and is not important for them to remember and understand. They feel overwhelmed by the amount of information. The solution is to teach students about text structure.

Each of the four most common text structures has a distinctive shape as well as a set of cueing words and phrases that help keep the reader oriented as she or he reads (see diagram on facing page).

Providing students with visual organizers that mirror the text helps them to learn to manage information.

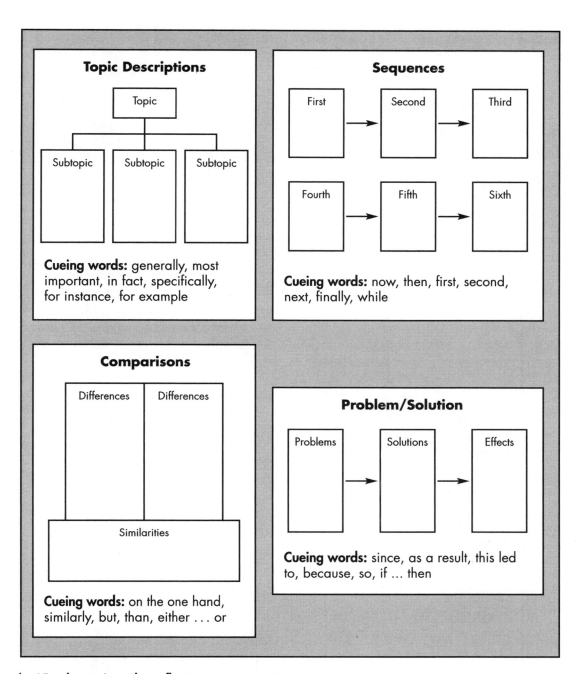

Topic Descriptions

Topic

Subtopic Subtopic Subtopic

Cueing words: generally, most important, in fact, specifically, for instance, for example

Sequences

First → Second → Third

Fourth → Fifth → Sixth

Cueing words: now, then, first, second, next, finally, while

Comparisons

Differences Differences

Similarities

Cueing words: on the one hand, similarly, but, than, either . . . or

Problem/Solution

Problems → Solutions → Effects

Cueing words: since, as a result, this led to, because, so, if . . . then

Visual organizers that reflect text-structure patterns

How to Use the Strategy

Use Organizers 1-B to 1-F on pages 22–26: "Topic Description Organizer," "Sequence Organizer," "Cycle Organizer," "Comparison Organizer," "Problem/Solution Organizer."

Incorporate the use of Graphic Organizers into your classroom using the following steps:

1. First, explain how graphic organizers work, their purpose, and how they can help students become better readers. Explain that there are several different ways of representing information and that the key to using graphic organizers is to find the organizer that best represents the text's structure.

2. Model what you expect students to do. Create a working model organizer on the board or an overhead and distribute corresponding organizers to students. (Refer to Organizers 1-B to 1-F for samples to use.) For your model and for students' initial practice, choose readings in which the content is familiar to all students (e.g., differences between summer and winter). Also make sure that the information lends itself to graphic representation.

3. Using your working model organizer, show students how to use their corresponding visual organizers to take notes. Allow them to work on their own while the model is still clear in their head.

4. Over time, as students master the process, introduce additional organizers and text structures. Model their uses and compare and contrast the different text structures to ensure students can tell the differences between them.

5. Provide students with practice identifying the various text structures and selecting the most appropriate organizer.

6. Encourage students to develop their own visual organizers to fit the organizational patterns of the texts they are reading. For example, one creative second-grade student developed the diagram organizer at the right to help him understand a reading on insects.

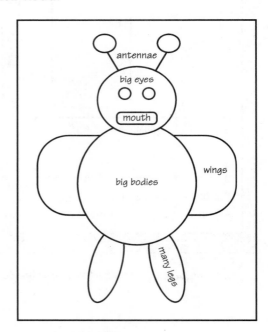

Diagram organizer

Helping the Struggling Reader

Research on graphic organizers shows that they are especially helpful to struggling students (Lehman, 1992). Nevertheless, students may require extra help in learning how to use them well.

Allow struggling readers to work with partners or in groups in which they can discuss their difficulties in using graphic organizers and can create a complete organizer collaboratively. Work with these groups to help students become aware of their own difficulties and to see what's involved in overcoming them. Allow other students in the group to explain what works for them when they run into difficulties.

You may also want to develop a list of problem-solving questions to guide students through the process and to help them internalize the steps. For example:

- How does the information seem to be arranged?
- Which organizer best matches the text's organization?
- What cueing words should I look for?
- What's the important information to write on the organizer?
- Does my completed organizer adequately summarize the reading(s)?

To help students develop confidence in using organizers, you may want to provide them with a word bank listing the words to be placed in the organizer. Because the students have access to the key words, the focus is taken off extracting relevant information and placed on using the concepts and the organizer appropriately. For instance, if your students are using a cycle organizer to understand a reading on the water cycle, you might provide them with key words and phrases such as:

- Vapor condenses
- Water evaporates and rises
- Vapor sticks to dust particles
- Billions of vapor droplets form clouds
- Earth's surface heats up
- Precipitation

This way, students build confidence in using the organizer.

Name: _____

Topic Description Organizer

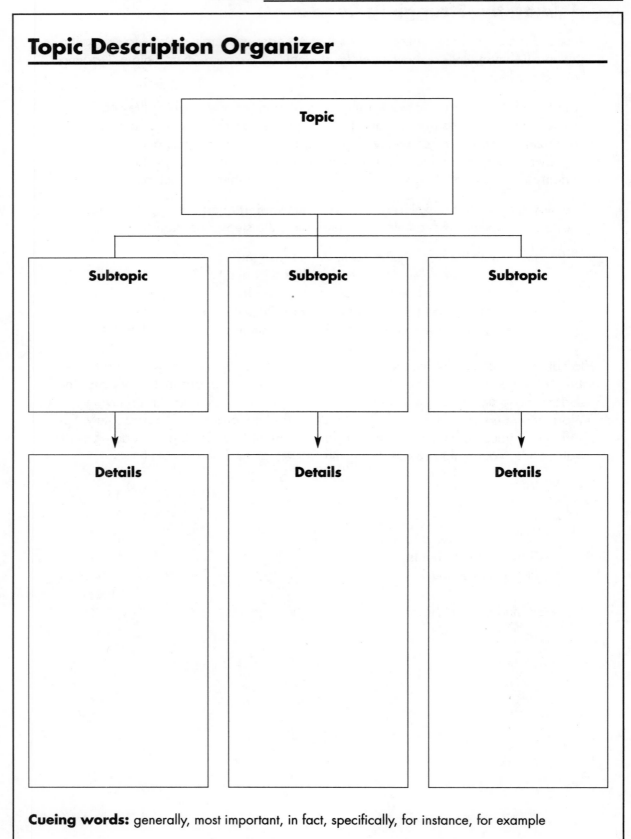

Cueing words: generally, most important, in fact, specifically, for instance, for example

Name: _____

Sequence Organizer

First	Second	Third

Fourth	Fifth	Sixth

Cueing words: now, then, first, second, next, finally, while

Name: _____

Cycle Organizer

Cueing words: now, then, next, finally, while, first, second

Name: _____

Comparison Organizer

Differences	Differences

Similarities

Cueing words: on the one hand, similarly, but, than, either . . . or

Name: _____

Problem/Solution Organizer

Problem	Solutions	Effects

Cueing words: since, as a result, this led to, because, so, if ... then

KNOW-WANT-LEARN (K-W-L)

The Strategy in Action

Every year, Carla Mitchell conducts an integrated math unit with her second graders on money. She begins her unit in a very interesting way: she distributes to each student a sealed envelope containing a single coin. Students are encouraged to feel the envelope and to guess what's inside. During this process of determining the envelope's contents, Carla asks her students to identify what they know about what's inside the envelope. By doing this, Carla provokes student curiosity and gets them thinking about the topic of the unit. Carla provides students with a Know-Want-Learn (K-W-L) organizer and then asks students to open their envelopes: Carla next says to her students, "Now that you know it's definitely money inside the envelope, think about everything you know about money. Try to think about lots of different times you've had or used money. Also, think about what you notice when adults use money."

Carla gives students time to write their ideas in the first column (What I Know) of their K-W-L organizer (top diagram) individually. Once students have completed their individual brainstorms, Carla engages the whole class in discussion and tallies the different ideas students have generated on a K-W-L poster (bottom diagram) she has posted in the front of the room.

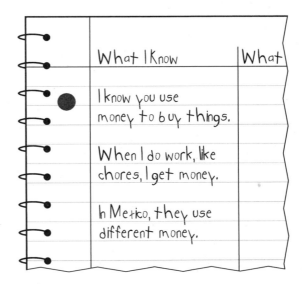

What I Know	What
I know you use money to buy things.	
When I do work, like chores, I get money.	
In Mexico, they use different money.	

Individual K-W-L organizer (1st column)

What We Know	What
1. People use money to buy things.	
2. Money is used in many places (stores, video games).	
3. When people do work, they are paid in money.	
4. People use symbols ($) and numbers to stand for money.	
5. Different countries use different money.	

Whole-class K-W-L poster (1st column)

What I Know	What I Want to Know
I know you use money to buy things.	How do people in stores know how to give you change so fast?
When I do work, like chores, I get money.	
In Metico, they use different money.	

Individual K-W-L organizer (2nd column)

What We Know	What We Want to Know
1. People use money to buy things.	1. How do people make change?
2. Money is used in many places (stores, video games).	2. Where does money come from?
3. When people do work, they are paid in money.	3. Why do different countries use different money?
4. People use symbols ($) and	

Whole-class K-W-L poster (2nd column)

"You really know a lot about money," Carla tells the class. "What other things would you like to know about money?" Once again, Carla allows time for individual response and uses a whole-class format to record questions and help all students process the ideas being discussed.

Once the class's questions have been recorded in the second column (What I Want to Know) of the students' organizers (top left diagram) and on the poster (top right diagram), Carla provides various activities to help students find answers to their questions. For example, to help students understand how to make change, Carla first models and coaches students through the skill of making change. She then helps student groups set up "learning stores" in which students play roles as customers, cashiers, and notetakers. After each student has "bought" a number of items, made change for student "customers," and observed the change-making process by taking notes, Carla pulls students together into groups. These groups examine and discuss their notes and then identify patterns they noticed in the "learning stores." Carla has each group create a chart (bottom diagram) displaying the patterns they noticed about making change.

Patterns for Making Change

1. When you buy something, you always get back less money than you started with.
2. There is sometimes more than one way to make the same change.
3. Four quarters make a dollar.
4. Two dimes and a nickel make a quarter.
5. Two nickels make a dime.
6. Five pennies make a nickel.

Student-created chart

To help students find answers to some of their other questions, Carla provides a range of learning opportunities in her unit (for example, a talk from a coin collector, books and articles about money in different cultures and civilizations). Throughout the unit, students add their discoveries to the third and final column of their K-W-L organizer. Carla conducts a final survey of the class's learnings and records responses on the class poster. After all responses have been recorded, Carla reviews the big ideas in the unit and asks students to reflect on their learning and the K-W-L process in their reflection logs.

*   *   *

Fourth-grade teacher Esteban Carr is using K-W-L in a more focused and more traditional way. He is using it in conjunction with a specific reading. Esteban has found that K-W-L can be made an even more powerful reading tool by making a slight modification to the organizer, which looks like this:

Before Reading		During Reading	After Reading	
What I Know	What I Think I Know	Big Ideas from Reading	What I Learned	What I Still Want to Learn

Modified K-W-L organizer

By dividing reading into before, during, and after phases, Esteban allows students to see how the reading process is layered and progressive.

Esteban is using K-W-L and his adapted organizer to help students make sense of a reading in *Ranger Rick* that describes the delicate balance of predator-prey relationships in ecosystems across the globe. Before reading the selection, students develop two lists: in the first list, they generate as many hunting animals or predators as they can; in the second, they list all the prey animals they know. In the first column of the K-W-L organizer, students use their prey/predator list to list all they know about predator-prey relationships. Esteban then asks students what they'd like to know about these relationships. Esteban models this questioning process by asking students to think about the kinds of questions a biologist or ecologist might ask while reading the article (for example, "What happens in an ecosystem when there are not enough prey animals to feed the predators?"). Esteban and the students decide on three questions they think are the most interesting:

1. What happens if an ecosystem doesn't have enough predators?
2. What happens if an ecosystem doesn't have enough prey animals?
3. Is hunting cruel?

Esteban divides the class into groups, each of which focuses its attention on one of the three questions above. Students read the article individually and take notes in the center column of the organizer (Big Ideas from Reading) that correspond to the question guiding their search. Student groups then convene to discuss their findings and create a list of the most important ideas. Throughout the reading phase, Esteban circulates around the room to make sure students are gathering appropriate information and working together productively.

Why the Strategy Is Beneficial

Research on reading has shown that the activation of prior knowledge is one of the most important skills for quality reading (Anderson & Pearson, 1984; Moore, Readence, & Rickelman, 1989). Expert readers know how to tap into their base of knowledge and use it to make sense of the readings they encounter. A number of years ago, in looking at the role of prior knowledge in building students' reading skills, Ogle (1986) developed K-W-L, which has since become one of the most popular and recognizable strategies in classrooms across the country.

In K-W-L, after the teacher introduces a topic, students use a "factstorming" technique (groups of 3–5 students generate as many facts as they can) to generate whatever they know about the topic. This process helps the teacher access students' prior knowledge and helps students use that background knowledge to make sense of the forthcoming reading.

After their fact-finding, students generate a list of what they would like to know about the topic, which provides a purpose for reading and a guide for information search. Then students read the text to verify their knowledge and to add to it by finding answers to their questions.

How to Use the Strategy

Use Organizers 1-G to 1-I on pages 34–36: "K-W-L," "K-W-L, Variation 1," or "K-W-L, Variation 2."

Incorporate the K-W-L strategy in your classroom using the following steps:

1. Introduce a topic to be studied or text to be read.
2. Distribute Organizer 1-G, "K-W-L," (or use variation organizers 1-H or 1-I) and explain what the initials stand for.
3. To access students' prior knowledge, have them use the first column of the organizer, "What I Know," to create individual lists of what they already know about the topic.
4. Have students meet in groups of 3–5 and use the "factstorming" technique to generate more ideas, share their findings and add to their personal lists.
5. Finally, conduct a whole-class discussion to further allow students to expand their lists. (This background knowledge will help students make sense of the forthcoming reading.)
6. Ask students to formulate a list of questions about what they want to know using the second column of the organizer ("What I Want to Know"). Encourage students to think openly and flexibly in generating this question "wish list," which will become the basis for determining what students think is important to know. The questions also provide students with a purpose for reading and a guide for their information search.
7. Have students read the text to verify their knowledge and to find answers to their questions, which they add to the third column ("What We Learned") on the organizer. (Questions not answered by the text may become the basis for independent research, group inquiries, or other kinds of research projects.)
8. Conduct a discussion in which students reflect upon what they have learned as a result of this process.

Variations on the Strategy

Richardson and Morgan (1997) find that relabeling the columns to "What I Already Know," "What I Now Know," and "What I Still Need to Know" more clearly emphasizes prior knowledge, what is known after reading, and what students still need to find out after the reading has taken place (see Organizer 1-H).

Another variation of the K-W-L technique is to organize the information like teacher Esteban Carr did, into Before Reading ("What I Know" and "What I Think I Know"); During Reading ("Big Ideas from Reading"); and After Reading ("What I Learned" and "What I Still Want to Learn"). This organizer helps students see the evolution of their learning more clearly and allows students to identify what they still want to know about their topic, thereby setting the stage for independent or group research projects (see Organizer 1-I).

Helping the Struggling Reader

Student difficulties with K-W-L fall into three categories:

1. Difficulties in accessing what is already known.
2. Difficulties in generating questions about the topic.
3. Difficulties in actively reading the text to find relevant information.

The first difficulty is often encountered by teachers who hear statements like this: "I don't know anything about crocodiles!" To help struggling readers, teachers can use simple, even obvious questions to activate prior knowledge. For instance, in response to the student who thinks he knows nothing about crocodiles, you might use questions like these:

"Are crocodiles as big as elephants?"

"No."

"Are they bigger than cats?"

"Yes."

"You do know something about their size then. Now, are crocodiles like any other animals you know of?"

"They're a lot like alligators."

"Good. That's something else you know. Do you know anything about where they live?"

"In the water."

"In the ocean?"

"No, in swamps, I think."

"Good. You know a lot more than you think about crocodiles."

For students who encounter difficulty in generating questions about a topic, it is a matter of helping them realize they have questions to ask. Sometimes students believe they already know a lot about a topic and their overconfidence can, in fact, become a detriment to curiosity and an inquiring attitude. For example, you might find the student who claims she already knows that reptiles lay eggs. By encouraging the student to look deeper into her knowledge base with probing questions like "How many eggs do they lay?" or "Yes, they lay eggs, but is there a reason they lay eggs instead of giving birth like mammals?", you encourage students to realize that they always have questions. They just need to look for them.

Third, struggling readers may encounter difficulty extracting the information that verifies their knowledge and provides answers to their questions. A variety of techniques can be used to help students overcome this problem.

Modeling: For the struggling reader and the confident reader alike, modeling the K-W-L process, especially the active reading phase, is essential if you expect students to use the strategy on their own. Show them how you read a text. List steps on the board and coach students through them. Use Think Alouds (using a sample text, describe your thinking about how you read a text aloud) and directed practice to help them internalize the skill. Coach students through their learning.

Read Aloud: After students have determined what they know and what they want to know, have them listen to the text as you read it aloud. Encourage them to develop images or draw pictures of the reading in their mind. Then have them read it on their own.

Collaborative Reading: Tap into the power of group learning by allowing students to work together. Each student in the group may be held responsible for finding one key piece of information rather than several. Or, use a strategy like Peer Reading (page 37) or Collaborative Summarizing (page 40) to help students read actively.

Multiple Inputs: Encourage students to use more than one text to gather information. If students want to read more, by all means, allow them to do it.

Post-It Notes: Instead of marking up a text, students can place Post-It notes in front of key ideas in the reading so that they can look back and locate essential information.

Name: _____

K-W-L

What I **Know**	What I **Want** to Know	What We **Learned**

Name: _____

K-W-L, Variation 1

What I Already Know	What I Now Know	What I Still Need to Know

Name: _____

K-W-L, Variation 2

Before Reading		During Reading	After Reading	
What I Know	What I Think I Know	Big Ideas from Reading	What I Learned	What I Still Need to Learn

PEER READING

The Strategy in Action

As part of their unit on natural disasters, Robert McGill's fourth graders are studying earthquakes. The students have been divided into pairs. Each student in each two-person team has a copy of an article about the causes and effects of earthquakes and the uncanny ability of some animals to predict coming earthquakes. The article has been divided into four short sections by Robert, and both members of each team have a coaching sheet (see diagram) with questions keyed to building a brief summary of each section of the reading. Morris, the A reader, will address questions 1, 4, and 5, while Sara, the B reader, will address questions 2, 3, and 6.

As Peer Reading partners, both Morris and Sara read each section independently, marking the text to highlight the information that feels important to them. At the end of the first section, both stop reading, and after taking a quick look at his marked text, Morris turns the article over so he can't see it. Sara keeps her copy of the article open and asks Morris question 1, "What causes earthquakes?" As he answers, Sara uses her marked text to coach him toward a more complete answer.

When he finishes, both read section two and then reverse roles. Sara puts her materials aside while Morris coaches her toward complete answers to the questions, "What happens during an earthquake?" and "What are the effects of earthquakes on people, animals, and the land?"

The partners continue this process of reading and coaching for sections three and four, reversing roles each time. After completing the reading,

---

Peer Reading Coaching Sheet

Section One Question (for reader A)

1. What causes earthquakes?

Section Two Questions (for reader B)

2. What happens during an earthquake?
3. What are the effects on people, animals, and the land?

Section Three Questions (for reader A)

4. What animals are the best earthquake predictors?
5. How do animals behave before earthquakes?

Section Four Question (for reader B)

6. What do scientists believe are the reasons animals can predict earthquakes?

Summarizing questions for guiding a reading

both students reread the article and use the question sheet to take notes that will help create a summary. Together, both students in the partnership then develop a comprehensive summary of the article (see diagram).

As students work, Robert circulates around the room. He takes notes on students' notetaking and summarizing behaviors, looking for strengths and weaknesses, and collecting data for his own record of students' development. Over the next few weeks, Robert will gradually teach his students to create their own summarizing questions, which they will use to conduct independent research into another natural disaster in human history and how people coped with it.

Earthquakes

Earthquakes come from cracks in the Earth called faults. Shock waves come from the fault and make the ground roll and shake. Earthquakes can make trees and buildings fall. Streets can crack and pipes can break. When things fall or break, people and animals can be hurt or killed.

Some animals seem to know when earthquakes will come. The best earthquake predictors are snakes, lizards, and small animals. They run out of their burrows before earthquakes. Other animals get angry before an earthquake or they get scared and bark. Scientists think animals can hear or sense changes in the Earth before earthquakes. Humans cannot sense these changes.

Student summary of article

Why the Strategy Is Beneficial

For many years, the teaching of summarizing involved teaching students how to:

1. Delete unnecessary ideas and details.
2. Replace specifics with more general ideas.
3. Select or construct main ideas or topic sentences from a text.

However, several problems plague this procedure. In 1986, Peter Afflerbach and Peter H. Johnston pointed out that the ability to delete trivial or unimportant information presumes that students know how to identify important information. Yet this is exactly the skill most average and below-average readers lack.

In addition, Afflerbach and Johnston noted that the construction of unstated main ideas constituted a second area of difficulty for struggling readers. Complicating the situation further is the fact that not all nonfiction passages are organized around a main idea and detail structure. Some describe a sequence, others discuss cause and effect, while still others compare information or tell a story. Asking students to search for main ideas when reading expository prose establishes a schema that may conflict with the organizational structure of the reading and thus hinder or obstruct comprehension. Finally, as Cunningham and Moore pointed out in 1986, asking students to read each passage and decide on its main idea tends to be vague and may not focus their attention on any specific information. On the other hand, readers with a concrete problem to solve, such as "What is the ocean floor like?" or "Why did the Roman Empire fall?" have a definite purpose that leads them to specific information.

With these ideas in mind, Silver, Hanson, Strong, and Schwartz (1996) developed a revised model of summarizing. In Silver and Strong's version, an informational text is an attempt to answer questions organized around a central topic. This approach to summarizing, called Peer Reading, yields four distinct advantages to the traditional teaching of summarizing:

1. The use of summarizing questions scaffolds the task of summarizing by directing students to specific information.
2. Both the oral summary and the presence of a coach heighten the processing of information and provide students with a greater sense of control over the reading.
3. Students process the text in four ways: by answering the questions, by coaching their partners, by taking notes, and by developing a collaborative summary.
4. Students work toward independence, eventually creating their own summarizing questions to build comprehension and as an independent research tool.

How to Use the Strategy

Use Organizer 1-J, "Peer Reading," on page 41.

You can incorporate the Peer Reading strategy in your classroom using a method similar to that employed in "The Strategy in Action Section."

1. Select a reading and break it up into manageable sections.
2. For each section, create a question or a set of questions that will require students to summarize the section. Write these questions on Organizer 1-J, "Peer Reading."
3. Break up students into pairs. Distribute the reading and the summarizing questions to all students.
4. Ask students to read the first section, mark their text, and then engage in coaching partnerships (reader A puts his reading aside while the coach asks the summarizing questions and uses his marked copy to coach reader A to a more complete answer).
5. Have students reverse roles for each remaining section of the text.
6. When they are finished, ask students to use the summarizing questions to take notes on the reading and then to create a summary collaboratively.
7. Over time, gradually model and coach students through the process of identifying their own summarizing questions and using their new skills to summarize readings and conduct research.

Helping the Struggling Reader

The teacher's observations, notetaking, and coaching of the individual student teams provide opportunities for diagnosing and interviewing students with particular problems that occur during the operation of the Peer Reading strategy.

For students who are still having difficulty summarizing the reading, the Collaborative Summarizing strategy (Silver, Strong, & Perini, in press) can be used. The strategy works like this:

1. After reading, students list three to five ideas they believe to be the most important.
2. Students pair up with a partner and review the guidelines for consensus negotiation:
   - Avoid win-lose statements.
   - Yield only to positions that have sound, logical foundations.
   - Avoid quick and easy solutions.

   Using these guidelines, students negotiate with their partner to reach consensus on the most important points in the reading(s).
3. Each student pair meets with another pair and the four students renegotiate their lists to create a comprehensive list of the most important points (top diagram). Once students have agreed upon their lists, the group prepares a collaborative summary.
4. The teams of four then meet with another team, read their summaries, and develop a set of agreed-upon criteria for powerful summaries (bottom diagram).
5. Groups share their criteria with the class and reflect upon their understanding of the content and what makes a good summary.
6. Students use these criteria to develop individual summaries of new readings they encounter.

Spanish Conquistadors

✔ The conquistadors were courageous.

✔ The conquistadors were extremely cruel to Native Americans.

✔ The conquistadors led expeditions to Central, South, and North America.

✔ The conquistadors wanted gold.

✔ Weapons and European diseases helped the conquistadors conquer the Native Americans.

A negotiated list of important points in the text

What Makes a Summary Powerful?

1. A powerful summary is accurate and thorough.
2. A powerful summary identifies main ideas and important details (unless a reading has a different pattern—then the summary should follow that pattern).
3. A powerful summary is clear and well organized.
4. A powerful summary correctly applies the rules of:
   - punctuation.
   - grammar.
   - spelling.
   - capitalization.

Negotiated criteria for developing powerful summaries

Name: _____

Peer Reading

Section 1 Question(s) (for Reader A)

Section 2 Question(s) (for Reader B)

Section 3 Question(s) (for Reader A)

Section 4 Question(s) (for Reader B)

RETELLING

The Strategy in Action

Amira DeKahn and his sixth-grade students have spent the last three weeks studying tales of discovery in their social studies class. In working their way through this unit, students have:

- Gathered in groups to conduct research around "shared books."
- Discussed what they learned with the whole class and the teacher.
- Brainstormed lists of everything they know about discovery and looked for patterns to organize their learning.

Today, Amira is going to introduce the Retelling strategy using a reading on Marco Polo and his travels through the Middle and Far East called "Discovering the Unknown East." He begins by telling his students the title of the reading and asking them to help him predict ideas the reading might contain as well as some of the words or vocabulary they would expect such a passage to use.

When the class has completed its list of predictions, Amira reads the passage aloud and then asks students to read it on their own silently. Amira then shows students how he continues to read and reread the passage until he knows he's ready to write a retelling of the reading in his own words. The students then work for 30 minutes or so, reading and writing their own retellings (see sample). The lesson closes with students sharing and comparing their retellings and discussing the differences they find in each other's work.

As the year goes on, Amira's students show a progressively better grasp of the content of their reading and greater maturity as writers. Every month their writing, as well as their approach to reading, becomes more organized, more insightful, more vivid.

> **Sample Retelling**
>
> In 1271 Marco Polo sailed with his father from Venice, Italy, to China at the age of fifteen. It took Marco and his father three years to reach China. When they got there, Marco impressed Kublai Khan, the ruler of China. Kublai Khan liked Marco so much that he made him one of his ambassadors. Marco spent the next seventeen years traveling to countries like India and Persia as the ambassador of Kublai Khan. Finally, in 1292, Marco and his father decided to leave China and return to Venice. It took them three years to get back home and Marco was now thirty-nine years old.

Retelling of a reading

Why the Strategy Is Beneficial

In 1987, Hazel Brown and Brian Cambourne (a primary school teacher and a researcher at the University of Wollongong in Australia, respectively) pioneered the

Retelling strategy as an effective technique for helping students develop listening, comprehension, and summarizing skills. The strategy they developed moves through five phases:

1. Immersion—students read texts with a common theme (discovery) or genre (fables).
2. Prediction—students predict topics, events, and vocabulary likely to appear in the text.
3. Reading—teacher reads the passage, then student reads the passage.
4. Retelling—student writes a retelling of the passage.
5. Share and Compare—students share their retellings, noting the differences.

Brown and Cambourne noted that the use of the Retelling strategy improved student comprehension markedly and that, unexpectedly, the strategy also precipitated the following general improvements in students' language skills:

- Students were using a greater variety of new sentence forms and structures in their writing.
- Students were showing greater confidence in their abilities to read, write, and understand.
- Students were making fewer spelling and punctuation errors.

Brown and Cambourne labeled these surprises *linguistic spillovers* to indicate that the effects they found had spilled over far beyond their initial setting within Retelling. Over time, these student improvements spread beyond the boundaries of the strategy and served to improve students' overall approach to a wide variety of reading and writing tasks.

The reason for this general improvement is twofold. First, by immersing students in a thematic or genre-based unit, students become less likely to see the strategy as isolated or occasional and instead begin to look for connections, relationships, and further applications of their skills and knowledge within the unit. Immersion also provides students with a context that maximizes their opportunities for using prior knowledge. The second reason for linguistic spillover lies in the post-reading task of creating a summative retelling. Borne out by a variety of researchers (Doctorow, Wittrock, & Marks, 1978; Morrow, 1983; Taylor & Beach, 1984), the fact is that when students are given post-reading tasks that are generative in nature (e.g., a summary, a retelling, an interpretation), their levels of retention and comprehension prove significantly higher than when they are asked to complete less-demanding post-reading tasks like multiple choice or end-of-chapter review questions.

What this research indicates is that demanding post-reading tasks such as creating a retelling will actually lead students to reorganize and refine their reading and writing processes. With modeling and practice, students will develop more flexible schemas that can be applied in many linguistic situations. This finding suggests that scaffolding students' reading by reducing task size to a minimum (e.g., multiple choice, matching exercises) may inhibit reading development.

How to Use the Strategy

Use Organizer 1-K, "Predict and Retell," on page 46.

Incorporate the Retelling strategy into your classroom using the following steps:

1. Ask students to use the title, bold print, or pictures of a text to generate a list of predictions in the space provided on Organizer 1-K, "Predict and Retell," about the topics, events, and vocabulary likely to appear in the text.
2. Read the text to the students so that they hear adult use of pauses and inflections, which enhances comprehension.
3. Now ask students to read the text silently on their own, as many times as necessary, in order to feel confident they can produce a retelling. Remind students that their goal is to understand, not to memorize verbatim.
4. Challenge students to write, in the space provided on the organizer (or on a separate page), a retelling of the passage, without looking back. Students should try to create a text of their own that could help other readers get the same pleasure and understanding they derived from the text.
5. Ask students to team up with a partner and share their retellings, noting differences in their presentation.
6. Encourage students to identify areas where they might have "muddled the meaning," examine differences in their use of paraphrasing, and discuss what they might "steal" from each other to improve their retellings.

Helping the Struggling Reader

Following are some solutions for struggling readers who run into four sources of difficulty with summarizing tasks.

The student lacks background knowledge. This problem is much less likely to occur if the retelling is embedded in a unit that explores reading texts linked by common theme or genre.

The student does not understand the way the text is structured. Immersion in texts linked by a common theme or genre is also useful here. However, text structure may continue to elude students. Graphic organizers may prove helpful by supplying students with various structures that they can superimpose on their readings to discover which structure fits. This activity can be explored in groups or alone and should revolve around the idea of structure in texts and why it is important. (For more information see Graphic Organizers, pages 16 to 26.)

The student does not see how to create a retelling out of the reading passage. Help students learn to manage this difficulty by modeling the process as extensively as possible. Pull together a small heterogeneous group (five to six students) that contains some adept readers and retellers along with some who are experiencing more difficulty. Show the group directly how you put together a retelling, emphasizing how you use structural clues within the piece ("See how each paragraph begins with a number word: 'first,' 'second,' etc."), and paraphrasing ("How might we say this sentence in another way using our own words?"). Then examine another text together and coach the group toward their own shared retelling. If your struggling readers continue to have difficulty, pull them aside for more systematic work on summarizing (see "Collaborative Summarizing," page 40).

The student does know what a good retelling looks like. Students will benefit greatly by seeing and analyzing exemplary retellings. Use superior retellings as models. Provide students with a double-input rubric both the student and the teacher can use to assess summaries. For example:

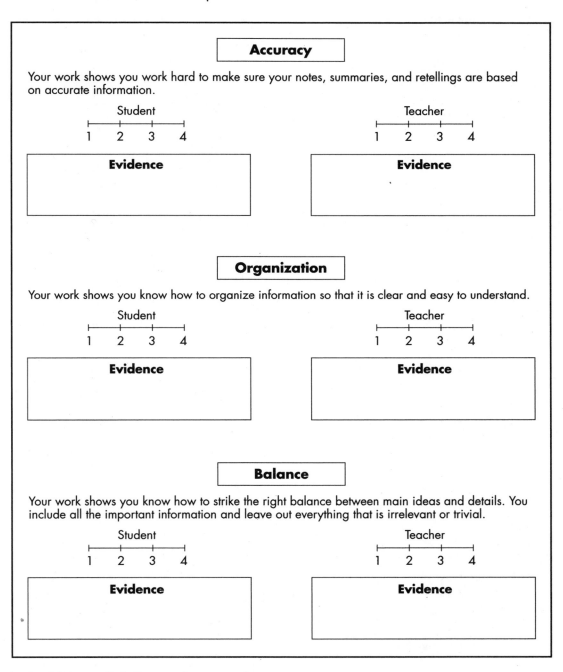

Double-input rubric for assessing summaries

Name: _____

Predict and Retell

Title of Reading: _____

_____

Predictions

Before you read the text, use the title of the reading, bold print, or pictures to make a list of predictions about the topics, ideas, events, and words or vocabulary that might appear.

_____

Retelling

After you have read the text, retell what you have read in your own words.

_____

Review

Re-read the text. Compare your retelling with the text. Ask yourself:

- Is my retelling accurate?
- Is it well organized?
- Does it show a balance between main ideas and details?

Now, check the box below that best describes your retelling:

☐ Excellent　　☐ Good　　☐ O.K.　　☐ Needs Help

SPLIT SCREEN

The Strategy in Action

In response to his state's new standards, Lester Grundley helps his students develop proficiency in listening skills and visual literacy with regular use of the Split Screen strategy. Today for science class, Lester is using Split Screen in conjunction with the class's learning unit on plants by reading *The Reasons for a Flower*, by Ruth Heller (1983).

To begin, Lester reads the book aloud. Students do not take notes; their only job is to listen. Sometimes, Lester stops reading to discuss difficult vocabulary words like "pollen" and "nectar" with his students to make sure that they understand what the words mean. Once Lester has completed reading the book, he reads it again. But this time, he reads it very slowly and with emphasized emotion. During this second reading, students write and sketch their ideas about the text on a form that looks like this:

Words (Ideas and Details)	Pictures (Sketches and Doodles—No Words)
birds butterflies bees drink nectar bring pollen help flower	

Written and sketched ideas about a reading

At key points in the text, Lester stops reading and asks students to explain their pictures to each other and to identify big ideas and important details with one another. After the second reading, Lester puts students into groups to create posters that tell the story of a flower.

Lester knows that Split Screen builds listening and visualizing skills. But he also knows it builds reading skills as well. In fact, by this time next month, Lester expects each of his students will be able to use Split Screen on their own as a tool to help them build visual images of the big ideas in their readings.

Why the Strategy Is Beneficial

Do you ever remember having a hard time with a reading because you couldn't see it? For example, did a passage on the way blood flows back and forth between the lungs and the valves and the chambers of the heart ever seem impossibly abstract to you? Similarly, much of children's difficulty lies in seeing or creating the right images for the processes they are studying. Even young children examining something as basic as a bean plant frequently have trouble with the concepts they need to master: Why is sunlight important? Where does the water go? What's the difference between pollen and seeds?

Split Screen (adapted from Seigel, 1984, and Brownlie, Close, & Wingren, 1990) is designed to help students see and refine the images they naturally create while reading and listening. The strategy works well for any reading (e.g., science, social studies, literature, math word problems) where images or imagery are important. It also works well as a notemaking procedure: the linguistic element facilitates the skill of separating essential and nonessential information while the visual component helps students summarize and condense information.

Research supports imaging and image-making as important skills used spontaneously by proficient readers (Keene & Zimmermann, 1997), yet most readers need both training and practice to become competent image makers (Pressley, 1977; Sadoski, 1985). Fortunately, the time needed for initial training need not take long: Pressley (1976) succeeded in teaching third graders to form images in twenty minutes while Gambrell and Bales (1986), working with struggling fourth and fifth graders successfully trained their students to create images in under thirty minutes.

How to Use the Strategy

Use Organizer 1-L, "Split Screen," on page 50.

Incorporate the Split Screen strategy into your classroom using the following steps:

1. Read a book or passage aloud while students listen. If the emphasis is to be placed on reading rather than listening, ask students to read the passage to themselves. Along the way, identify and discuss difficult vocabulary words.
2. Distribute a Split Screen organizer (Organizer 1-L) to each student. Tell students that you will reread the passage aloud, and that they are to take notes and draw pictures or icons to represent ideas. Encourage sketches over refined scenes.
3. Now reread (or have students reread) the passage aloud slowly and with emphasized emotion so that pauses, inflections, and tones are more easily used as cueing devices. Pause during rereading to give students time to create their visualizations on the organizer.

4. Ask students to pair or team up to explain their pictures and to identify big ideas and important details.
5. Have students work together or in pairs to create a product (e.g., a poster, an organizer) that uses both words and pictures to explain and summarize the reading. If the passage describes a sequence or procedure, encourage students to use a comic book format—one frame for every step in the process.
6. Encourage students to use Split Screen as an independent notemaking technique.

Helping the Struggling Reader

The ability to visualize information enhances and improves reading. Good readers form mental images in their heads to better understand the material and to improve their ability to recall details later. This vital skill can be difficult for many readers, particularly when working with image-laden passages. Below are some ways to help struggling image-makers.

- **Progressive Imaging:** Begin with younger students by showing them how to create images for words, then sentences, then paragraphs, and then larger passages.
    Word—Can you think of an image that represents "love"?
    Sentence—Can you draw a picture for this sentence? "Alligators have rough, scaly skin, powerful jaws, and long tails."
    And so on.
- **Icons:** Discuss icons that students are familiar with (No Smoking signs, restroom gender markers) and how they are useful. Show students how icons are helpful as a shorthand when taking notes and discuss their value in helping students remember ideas from reading.
- **Visualizing Questions:** The right questions can help guide students to visualize information. For instance, asking students to think of things they know that are rough or scaly can help them imagine what an alligator's skin looks and feels like.
- Use the Mind's Eye strategy on pages 103 to 105 to help students build visual skills.

Name: _____

Split Screen

Notes About the Text

Pictures, Symbols, Icons	Big Ideas, Important Details
Pictures, Symbols, Icons	Big Ideas, Important Details
Pictures, Symbols, Icons	Big Ideas, Important Details

Chapter Two

From Notetaking to Notemaking

Chapter Overview: Advance Organizer

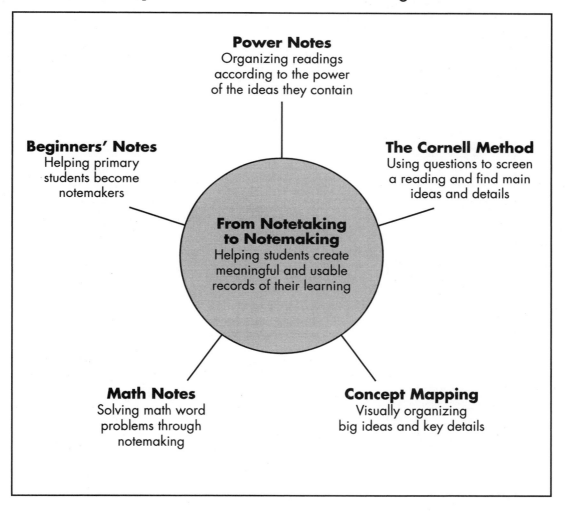

Power Notes
Organizing readings according to the power of the ideas they contain

Beginners' Notes
Helping primary students become notemakers

The Cornell Method
Using questions to screen a reading and find main ideas and details

From Notetaking to Notemaking
Helping students create meaningful and usable records of their learning

Math Notes
Solving math word problems through notemaking

Concept Mapping
Visually organizing big ideas and key details

> *"I want my notes to be tools for thinking."*
>
> Lucy Calkins
> Author, *Living Between the Lines*

Why Are Notes So Important?

Ask the average teacher, the average parent, the average American, "Is notetaking an important skill?" and they will probably answer "Yes" all the way down the line. Most would probably say they want it taught in schools, they want it to be an important part of the curriculum, and they want students to become proficient in taking notes. This is the answer we expect and hope for, and for very good reasons. Consider for a moment what you can't do if you can't take notes:

1. You can't conduct research effectively.
2. You can't keep track of the main ideas and important details in your textbook.
3. You can't remember in October what you read and learned in May.
4. You can't trace themes, patterns, and ideas that run through a month or a year.
5. You can't plan effectively for long-range projects.
6. You can't practice condensing and compacting information and deciphering what is and is not important in what you read.
7. You can't collect ideas from different sources and perspectives and see how they relate.
8. You can't keep track of the thoughts and questions that occur to you as you read.
9. You can't personalize your learning, keep a record of what it means to you, or return to ideas and questions you've had before and use them as sources for new books to read, new projects to pursue, or new pieces to write.
10. Eventually, maybe not today or tomorrow, but sometime—in middle or high school, in college or on your first or your third job, you won't be able to learn something as well as someone who knows how to take good notes.

Results of inability to take notes

Found Pets, Kitchen Sinks, and Notes

As important as notes are to many people, notes and notebooks are a bit like found pets and kitchen sinks: lots of people think they're a good idea but it's hard to find anyone who wants to care for them. Many students might like to buy new notebooks and decorate them, but few enjoy taking care of what's inside them. Similarly, many adults view notetaking as part of the drudgery of learning, associating it with the hours they lost copying from the board, paraphrasing articles from an encyclopedia, and scurrying their pens over lined paper trying to catch up to a professor's last words. Many teachers dislike teaching notetaking as well. In fact, many teachers see teaching the skill as a struggle whose only joy is in seeing student papers that are neat and organized. All of this brings us back to where we started: almost everyone agrees notes are an essential but repetitive and routine task. But what if everyone's wrong? What if taking notes is a deep and dynamic form of thinking? What if taking notes is a personal and creative act?

Notetaking to Notemaking

Take note: notemaking is a deeply creative act of learning. If this simple fact is difficult for most people to see—from the student who likes the notebook's colorful cover but not its insides, to the adult remembering impossibly long lectures with professors who spoke like machine guns, to the teacher feeling that vague sense of dread while preparing to teach students how to take notes—it is probably because they have never *made* notes. All of them have spent hours upon hours "notetaking." Notemaking is something else entirely. Let's listen to three people who know the difference between notetaking and notemaking:

> "How could anyone ever get bored with notemaking? There are so many different ways to make notes. And then there's figuring out which way works best in which situation. We talk about it all year long."
>
> *Stan Silverman*
> *Third-Grade Teacher*

> "I begin the year with notemaking. Notes are what young children write. They make these little marks on the page and when you ask them what they mean they tell you worlds. Worlds in just a little mark or scribble."
>
> *Maddy Lefferts*
> *Primary school teacher*

> "Without my notebooks, I'd be lost. My whole year, everything I learned, is in there. Notes help me a lot. We have to create a one-act play about people in the Depression. My group was using the textbook plus some sources from the library to get ready. So I suggested to my group that we make Concept Maps to keep track of our ideas. It's great—we put "Depression" in the middle and the ideas just kept coming. Soon, our whole project was organized for us."
>
> *Yan Huo*
> *Fifth-Grade Student*

Descriptions of the notemaking technique

Maddy, Stan, and Yan have very different ideas about notes than the people we described earlier. Maddy, Stan, and Yan understand that there are different noting techniques that make reading more meaningful. They know how notes can and should produce a personal, abbreviated text that mirrors the big ideas in the texts they read. No, Maddy, Stan, and Yan do not believe in taking notes; they believe in *making* them. What these three know implicitly is that notemaking is an extremely important skill for three reasons:

1. Through the act of notemaking, students create a shorter, more personal record of their own learning to which they can return to recall, rehearse, and revisit yesterday's learning.
2. The very act of notemaking requires students to consider a text more deeply in elaborating and developing its personal and literal meanings.
3. The process of notemaking is a far more appropriate method of practicing and applying comprehension skills than traditional worksheets or after-chapter questions.

To become good notemakers students need:

- A variety of techniques for recording and rewriting important information in the texts they read.
- The ability to separate the significant from the insignificant.
- A feel for what notemaking tools work best for them in different situations.

In this chapter, we will describe a variety of notemaking tools that students can use to deepen meaning and to build a record of learning.

Before we lay out these specific tools, let's take a moment to explore how students learn notemaking tools in general. Notemaking tools, like comprehension strategies, are best acquired through a three-step learning cycle.

Step One
The teacher models the process by thinking aloud, letting students see how her mind works as she approaches the task.

How it sounds in the classroom
"First, I skim the passage trying to get a general sense of what kinds of questions the text is trying to answer. So when I come to a subheading like this, I try to rewrite it as a question."

Step Two
The teacher asks students to practice using a notemaking tool on texts they have selected to fit their own interests or a common text that is part of their current study. As the students work, the teacher circulates, observing and coaching students and helping them adapt the strategies to their own situation and their own personal style.

How it sounds in the classroom
"You know, I often have trouble coming up with good questions as I read or skim my texts, so here's a little trick I use ..."

Step Three
The teacher regularly pulls the whole class together to discuss their adaptations and the problems they faced while trying to apply the techniques to their own reading.

How it sounds in the classroom
"In the beginning I was having trouble finding out what was really important. Then I remembered what you showed us about drawing our ideas. I found that if I sketched out my ideas first, it helped me see what was really important."

Three-step learning cycle for notemaking

By moving back and forth between modeling, practice, coaching, and discussions of application, the teacher helps the students adjust and adapt particular notemaking tools to their own personal styles and to the demands of different texts and research situations.

In the following pages, five teachers introduce their favorite notemaking tools and discuss how they use these tools to help their students become successful notemakers. This chapter of the book is similar to the previous one in that each notemaking tool is divided into four sections: The Notemaking Tool in Action, Why the Notemaking Tool Is Beneficial, How to Use the Notemaking Tool, and Helping the Struggling Notemaker. In the first of these four sections, The Notemaking Tool in Action, however, each teacher speaks in the first person about his or her experiences with the notemaking tool, while sample student notes appear with each teacher's discussion.

The five notemaking tools discussed are:

Beginners' Notes, which helps primary students learn to create simple notes.

Power Notes, which assists students in organizing their notes, from the main idea to specific details.

The Cornell Method, which calls for students to create questions about a reading, then to find details and main ideas that answer the questions.

Concept Mapping, which helps students group information and see connections.

Math Notes, which helps students analyze word problems before they begin solving them.

BEGINNERS' NOTES

The Notemaking Tool in Action

Mary Daley says that students need to learn how to take notes early, as part of their learning, not as an isolated skill. Here's how she does it with her primary students.

"In September, I introduce my students to notemaking by discussing the ways people make memories. Students talk about diaries, photographs, and videos. Then I explain that notemaking also is a way to make memories. To demonstrate this, I ask students at the end of the day to review what they learned and what they did, and to use words and pictures to record and list what they remember. Students share their lists with their parents to see how the notes have helped them make memories. For the rest of September we focus on making simple lists. Often, we'll brainstorm lists together: colors, toys, animals, holidays, etc. During brainstorms, I write students' ideas on the board, or I draw a picture of the idea. Sometimes, we also look for ways to group our notes, like circling all the winter holidays or putting a star next to all the animals that are pets.

"By October, students are making their own lists, and that means it's time to teach them how to find notes in their reading. For example, as they read stories and books they list things like the places Pooh goes, the way Frances shows she loves her little sister, or the types of foods that the pilgrims ate at the first Thanksgiving. Again, we often look for ways to group information they list. By the end of the month, students can usually make fairly comprehensive lists from their reading.

"By November, we've already talked quite a bit about how information can be grouped, so now students are ready to learn how to systematically organize information using concept webs. While creating basic webs with my students on topics such as what makes a good friend, I see lightbulbs lighting up in their heads. Suddenly, they get it—they see how lots of information can be chunked. Sometimes, students ask if they can go back to old lists and make concept webs out of those.

"Once students are comfortable making simple webs, we use what we've learned for a whole-class investigation. This year, we took a field trip to the local maritime museum. To prepare for our trip, I read two books about the seaside and we brainstormed and listed things we could investigate at the museum using words and pictures.

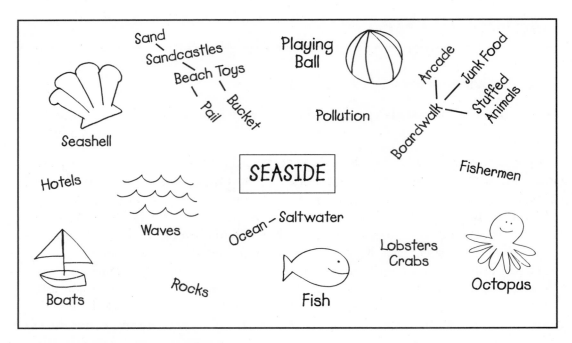

Sample of Beginners' Notes technique

"Students formed groups and used their lists to create concept webs as I walked around the room and helped them. From the webs the groups created, the class came up with three topics for investigation: animals at the seaside, businesses at the seaside, and people at the seaside. Each group took notes on one of these topics. When we got back, the groups looked through their notes to find as much information as they could about their topics. Each group created a collage of words, drawings, and clippings from the museum pamphlets. They had a great time, and so did I!"

Why the Notemaking Tool Is Beneficial

Notemaking is teaching students to create a record of their learning so they can look back, remember, and use what they know. Although study skills, including notemaking, have traditionally been reserved for older students, first grade or even kindergarten is the ideal time to begin building notemaking skills, which will become essential to student success in higher grades.

Based on Bobbi Fisher's (1995) work with primary students, Beginners' Notes follow a progressive structure that allows students to build skills over several months and then apply their new skills to an inquiry-based project. The notes that students create need not be too detailed and can include both simple words and pictures. As they practice and develop their skills of listing, finding information in books, making concept webs, and using notes for research, students continually share ideas with partners. This collaboration helps students get better at recognizing what important information looks like.

Students' abilities to become novice notemakers depends a great deal on their prior knowledge of the subject they are studying. For example, many students, after developing basic skills, will feel comfortable making notes about clothing or a book about dogs, but will not have the knowledge base to make notes on Native Americans if the topic is new to them. However, if the teacher directs and focuses a brainstorming activity, reads a book aloud, and shows a cartoon about Native American life, students will develop the knowledge needed to create and organize notes. Incorporating notes into a learning unit in this manner also will help students gain confidence in their ability to make notes.

How to Use the Notemaking Tool

Beginners' Notes entail a progressive plan to build student competence in notemaking through slow and gradual steps. Incorporate the tool into your classroom using these suggested steps:

Lists (September)
1. Introduce notemaking by explaining to students that they are going to "make memories."
2. Challenge students to list all the things they can think of for a category or topic. Direct the brainstorming and write each idea on the board for students to see and include on their own lists.
3. Encourage students to draw simple pictures as well as to use words. Include pictures on the board so students feel comfortable sketching ideas. Label sketches to foster vocabulary development.
4. After generating a list, work with students to find ways to identify related items (e.g., a list of foods can be broken into vegetables, meats, dessert foods). Have students record the relationships as you write them on the board.

Notes from Books (October)
1. Read a book aloud to the class.
2. Lead students in making notes on different kinds of information contained in the book (e.g., buildings in a community, people in a community, things in a community).
3. Ask students to make notes individually as you write on the board. Over time, students should begin to make notes on their own or in groups, using simple picture books.
4. Ask students to share notes in groups to help them fill in the gaps and identify missing information from their notes.

Concept Webs (November)
1. Introduce students to concept webs by webbing a simple, controlled topic like seasons. (If you need help with this step, see Concept Mapping, page 67). Explain that webs let us see how information can be organized.
2. Move toward webbing broader topics, using Organizer 2-B, "Concept Map," on page 69, or a simplified version. Here are two ideas for using concept webs.

- Tell the class the topic is clothes. Ask students to list different types of clothing, which you or a student can write on one side of the board. When a dead end is reached, ask a question like, "Why do people wear clothes when other animals don't?" Ideas about warmth, modesty, and not having any fur or feathers may arise, and these ideas can be written on another section of the board. This can be continued for a number of topics.
- Another possibility is to scatter ideas from the brainstorm randomly across the board and then draw lines to connect related ideas (e.g., for a foods brainstorm, dessert foods could be connected with yellow lines, meats with white lines). Students can then turn these into more comprehensive webs using the organizer.

Culminating Projects (when students are ready)
1. Provide questions or a topic organizer to help students see large categories (e.g., "What did you learn about the Colonists? Native Americans? The first Thanksgiving?") that they will use to structure their group project.
2. Ask students to organize ideas from one set of notes or combine and organize several sets. Advise group members to help each other fit information into the categories and fill gaps in their notes.
3. Have students use the newly organized notes to complete a group project such as a collage, poster, skit, or newspaper.
4. As students' skills develop, guide them in using more advanced notemaking techniques (e.g., bullets, numbering, Power Notes [page 61], Concept Mapping [page 67]) to organize their learning.

Helping the Struggling Notemaker

Even at this early stage, struggling notemakers can be helped using these methods:

Retelling: Ask a student who is struggling with identifying what to draw or write down to orally retell what happened in a story or picture book before taking his or her notes.

Questions: Overly detailed or random notes can be focused with questions. Before reading a book about tigers, for example, tell students you want them to take notes afterwards. Ask them to concentrate on three questions: "What do tigers look like? What do tigers eat? Where do tigers live?" Or, you may also want to ask students what they want to learn about tigers, and choose a few of their questions to focus on before reading.

Cooperative Learning: Have timid or confused notemakers work in groups while taking notes or during an encompassing project. Seeing the work of others helps them notice what details they may have missed or included mistakenly.

POWER NOTES

The Notemaking Tool in Action

Fourth-grade teacher Jim Aacker teaches his students how to become independent users of a technique called Power Notes.

"I like to introduce Power Notes to my students using basic concepts. For example, I usually teach the technique to students using something like sports as a model. After I write "Sports" on the board, I say, "Sports is our topic. What are some sports?" The kids rattle off a half dozen sports and I write them on the board, explaining that each one is a power one topic called "types of sports." Then, we look at a specific sport like baseball and I ask students for some ideas that would fit under that sport. After I get a number of responses like "bat, ball, glove," I write them beneath baseball, and so on, until we have a complete set of Power Notes for sports.

"By January, my students are creating elaborate Roman numeral outlines—without Roman numerals."

Reading Passage:	Student's Power Notes

While Native Americans wore highly decorated clothes for special occasions, they usually wore simple clothes for everyday use. They designed their clothes to suit their climate, from rainforests to deserts, where they wore clothes as a way to keep cool. Native Americans' clothes were also designed to be loose so that they could move more easily. Men usually wore shirts, loincloths, leggings, and tunics. Women wore skirts and dresses.	Topic: Native American Clothes
	
	1. Everyday clothes
	  2. Dressed to suit climate
	    3. rain forest
	    3. desert
	      4. wore very little, to keep cool
	  2. Clothes fit loosely for movement
	    3. men wore
	      4. loincloth
	      4. shirt
	      4. tunic
	      4. leggings
	    3. Women wore
	      4. skirts
	      4. dresses

Often, people wonder how Native Americans made all their clothes. Native Americans used the things around them to make their clothes. From animals, they used skin for cloth, sinews to make thread, and bones as needles. They also wove cloth from special kinds of plants . . .	1. How they were made
	  2. From things around them
	    3. Animals
	      4. skin for cloth
	      4. sinews for threads
	      4. bones for needles
	    3. Plants
	      4. wove cloth from

Sample of Power Notes technique

Why the Notemaking Tool Is Beneficial

Power Notes teach students the essential skills of extracting and discriminating between main ideas and the details that support them (Sparks, 1982). By breaking down textual information into various levels or "powers" of specificity, students produce a set of highly organized notes. Unlike traditional Roman numeral outlining, which requires students to remember a complicated organizational system, Power Notes are simple for students to learn and use: the only components students must remember are the numbers 1, 2, 3, and 4.

In a set of Power Notes, the ideas that most closely connect to the topic of a reading are the Power 1 ideas, or the main ideas. Powers 2, 3, and 4 designate information that is increasingly specific. For instance, if the topic of a passage is "outer space," a set of simple Power Notes might look like the diagram at the right.

Because Power Notes produce such a highly organized set of information, they are an ideal method for teaching students how to bring structure to their reading as well as to their writing tasks and study sessions.

Topic: Outer Space

Power 1:   Solar systems
   Power 2:   Planets
      Power 3:   Earth
             Mars
             Venus
         Power 4:   Resolve around stars
                  Usually have moons
                  Don't give off light
   Power 2:   Stars
      Power 3:   Sun
             North Star
         Power 4:   Give off light
                  Give off heat
                  Very large

Sample of Power Notes technique

How to Use the Notemaking Tool

Incorporate Power Notes into your classroom using the following steps:

1. Model Power Notes with your students, starting with well-known topics that have clear structures. You may begin by showing students an example such as the one on outer space, above.
2. Clarify the concept of powers by adding more levels with students. For instance, as new items such as "asteroids" and "black holes" are generated, ask students to determine which power they belong to and to explain why.

3. To further model the strategy, ask students to generate and organize sets of Power Notes as a class. Use well-known topics such as games, hobbies, movies, seasons, etc., and write class-generated Power Notes on the board (see diagram at right).
4. Move students to using Power Notes on their own as a way of organizing their reading.

Topic: Food

1. Mexican food
1. Fast food
1. Italian food
    2. pasta
        3. lasagna
           spaghetti
           ravioli . . . etc.

Introducing Power Notes using well-known topics

Helping the Struggling Notemaker

The most difficult aspect students encounter in learning Power Notes is learning how to organize information according to the tool's structure. Santa, Havens, and Maycumber (1996) make several suggestions for helping students overcome this difficulty.

1. Use class challenges in which you put two blank Power Notes structures on the board, provide a topic, and ask teams to compete against each other by filling in the blanks as quickly as possible.
2. Ask students to arrange index cards on which you have written power 1, 2, 3, and 4 words. Or, give each student in a group a single card and ask students to physically arrange themselves into 1, 2, 3, or 4 ideas.
3. Start with simple 1 and 2 power structures. Add 3 and 4 ideas as students' skills become more sophisticated. As skills develop, have students use their Power Notes to create written or spoken paraphrases of the original text.
4. Practice selective underlining with students by showing them how to underline key words and ideas and to assign each underline a power based on its relationship to the main idea.
5. Place a selected portion of text on an overhead. Model the process of creating Power Notes using Think Alouds (explaining your thinking process as you model the tool), selective underlining, and text marking.

THE CORNELL METHOD

The Notemaking Tool In Action

Roger Dixon, a fifth-grade teacher, says he's always been partial to the Cornell Method, a simple way of reinforcing good reading and study habits.

"In my class, first we skim the text to get a sense of the topics and subtopics. Then we convert these into questions. For example, if the heading says "Parts of the Circulatory System," we write, "What are the parts of the circulatory system?" in the left-hand column of the organizer. Then we read the passage and jot down the details and main ideas that answer our questions in the corresponding columns. I make sure that students are just writing down words and phrases—never sentences and never straight copying.

"When it comes time to study, the students just cover up the main idea and supporting details columns and there are the questions they need to know for the test, along with the answers. When students are unsure, they peek at the answers they created for themselves. After students have practiced answering the questions without looking at their notes, they put a '✓' next to the question if they know the answer, a '?' if they have a question about it, and a '*' if they need more review."

Parts of the Circulatory System		
Questions	**Details**	**Main Idea**
What are the parts of the circulatory system?	Heart—pump Arteries—carry blood out Veins—bring blood back Blood—nourishes body, contains oxygen	All parts work together to nourish body

Sample of the Cornell Method notemaking tool

Why the Notemaking Tool Is Beneficial

The main idea/detail format of the Cornell Method (Pauk, 1974) is especially effective with expository texts where the information is fairly well organized and the goal is for students to master the information. The Cornell Method organizer also makes a great tool for studying and reviewing. By adapting the strategy to include an extra column for questions as Roger Dixon did above, students learn how to direct their search for specific information in a text.

How to Use the Notemaking Tool

Use Organizer 2-A, "Cornell Method," on page 66.

Incorporate the Cornell Method into your classroom using the following steps:

1. Guide students in surveying the text for topics and subtopics.
2. Show students how to convert topics and subtopics into questions. Have students write their questions in the Questions column of Organizer 2-A, "Cornell Method."
3. Have students read the text and stop periodically to collect details and main ideas that answer the corresponding questions.
4. When they have completed a full set of notes, have students review their notes.
5. Ask students to cover up the details and main idea columns and to answer each question in their own words.
6. After students have reviewed their notes, allow them to assess their understanding using the following reader's punctuation:
   - ✔ I know this.
   - ? I have a question about this.
   - * I need to review this more.
7. Once students have taken a test or applied their learning to a synthesis task, have them reflect on the process. You can do this with questions like: "How well did you do on your test? Did the Cornell Method help you? What did you do to learn the material?"

   For example, in Darlene Freeman's third-grade class, students were asked to reflect on the process by restating all they did to prepare for the test. Darlene kept track of the responses on the board:
   1. We figured out how the author organized the text.
   2. We identified critical questions.
   3. We scanned the text for main ideas and details.
   4. We studied our notes by testing ourselves.
   5. We predicted the types of questions that would probably be asked on the test.

   After listing the students' reflections, Darlene asked them what ideas they would use to study for their next test.

Helping the Struggling Notemaker

If students have difficulty identifying main ideas and important details, practice the Main Idea strategy to help students learn how to find key words, main ideas, and supporting details. (See Main Idea, pages 11 to 15.)

Name: _____

Cornell Method

Self-Assessment	Questions	Details	Main Idea

✓   I know this
 ?   I have a question
     about this
 *   I need to review
     this more			

CONCEPT MAPPING

The Notemaking Tool in Action

"I guess concept mapping is as old as the hills," says teacher Janice Zatricia, "but it really works when my third graders have trouble seeing how information is related and grouped into topics, subtopics, and details. The strange thing is, every time we use it, I seem to learn something new about how it works.

"We begin by placing our topic in the center of the paper. Then we draw lines out from that for subtopics or questions we want to explore. As we gather details and main ideas from the reading, we connect them to their subtopic or question.

"Lately, we've added a new wrinkle: when their maps are finished, I ask my students to draw lines connecting details under one subtopic to details under another. I ask the students to label this relationship by writing down on the line what led them to make this connection."

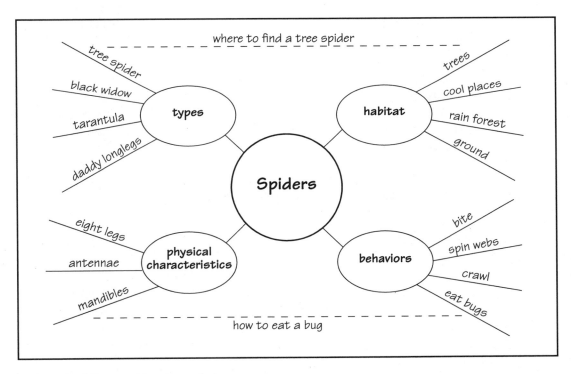

Sample of Concept Mapping technique

Why the Notemaking Tool Is Beneficial

Maps force students to pay attention as they read, reread, and study. Muth (1987) reports that mapping, because it makes hierarchical patterns of texts explicit, has proven to be highly successful in helping students manage expository reading tasks.

As a diagram, a map is a visual learning tool that capitalizes on spatial intelligence, promotes visual literacy, and supports right-brain activity. For students who tend to get lost in their reading, a map provides a way for them to see the text and its inner relationships in their entirety. Maps are especially helpful to younger students for this reason.

How to Use the Notemaking Tool

Use Organizer 2-B, "Concept Map" on page 69.

Incorporate Concept Mapping into your classroom using the following steps:

1. Identify a topic, main idea, or central question relevant to a reading or unit. Ask students to use Organizer 2-B, "Concept Map," to write this central idea in the circle at the center of the organizer.
2. With your students, identify secondary categories they would like to explore and have them connect the categories to the main idea, using the spaces provided on the organizer. (They can add circles as needed.) Model the process and describe your thinking as you identify the subtopics and details.
3. Guide students in using this "conceptual skeleton" to collect supporting details as they read. Show them how to connect each supporting detail to the subtopic it supports. (Students can add lines as needed.)
4. Students may then add to this map with further readings, explore connections between details, or use it as an aid for studying and recalling information.
5. Allows students to practice using concept maps on their own as a way to organize their readings.

Helping the Struggling Notemaker

Similar to other forms of notemaking, the most difficult aspect of mapping is for students to identify a reading's structure, topics, subtopics, and details. Here are some helpful ideas:

- Provide maps in which subtopics are already established for the students.
- Have students work collaboratively before working independently to help them build confidence.
- Provide generic concept maps for students to record their ideas, or use computer software that allows students to create their own mind maps.
- To stimulate hands-on, kinesthetic learning, have students create three-dimensional concept maps in the form of mobiles or sculptures.

Name: _____

Concept Map

Note: Feel free to add lines or circles as needed.

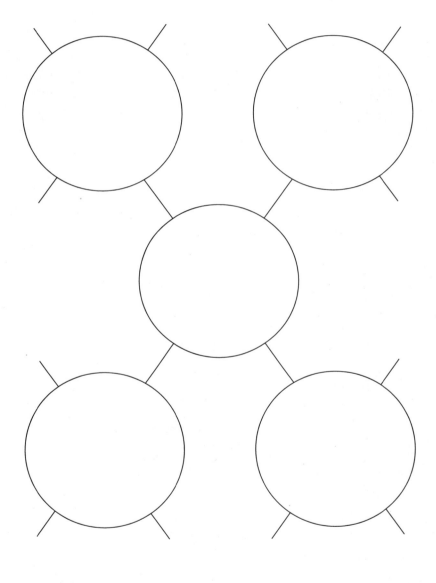

MATH NOTES

The Notemaking Tool in Action

Fifth-grade teacher Sarah Shays says, "My students have a lot of trouble coming to grips with word problems, so we use a simple window to help them take notes and deepen their reading and understanding of math problems.

"We begin by listing the relevant facts in the upper left hand corner of the window. Then we restate the problem in the lower left box and draw a picture or diagram in the lower right. Finally, we list the steps we are going to follow in the upper right-hand corner. Then we solve the problem on the back.

"My students keep their sheet in a special section of their notebook. That way when they get stuck, they can go back and leaf through problems they have already solved and see if they have ever solved a problem like the one they're stuck on."

The Facts	**The Steps**
What are the facts? • Cars hold four people. • Vans hold six people. What is missing? • Number of kids in class. • Number of cars and vans the class needs.	What steps can we take to solve the problem? • Find out how many people are going on the trip. • See how many will fit in vans because vans hold more people and less cars make less pollution for the environment. • Put the leftovers in cars. • Count the number of vehicles we used.
The Question	**The Diagram**

What question needs to be answered?
• How many cars and vans does our class need?
 	
Are there any hidden questions that need to be answered?
• How many people are going on the trip?
• Are empty seats okay?
• Should each vehicle be full?
	How can we represent the problem visually?
	
	    🚗 = 4
	
	    🧍 = 20
	
	    🚌 = 6

| *Sample of Math Notes technique*

Why the Notemaking Tool Is Beneficial

The introduction of word problems into the math curriculum represents a major shift in the way we ask students to think about math. Unlike the algorithmic nature of adding, subtracting, multiplying, and dividing, word problems require students to think analytically and to become problem-solvers rather than problem-doers.

Suddenly, for the student being introduced to word problems, math involves reading, determining the problem for oneself, identifying the problem's components, and developing a problem-solving plan—all new skills for most elementary students. These new and complex operations can be a source of anxiety and frustration for many students (Thomas, 1998) even as they are becoming increasingly central in most states' standards and assessments.

Math Notes, which are adapted from Thomas's Problem-Solving Strategy (1998), provide students with a systematic means of analyzing, dissecting, visualizing, and solving word problems. Since state standards and the National Council of Teachers of Mathematics recognize the need for students to reason their way through non-routine problems based on real-world contexts, it is essential that students are taught early on how to become strategic problem-solvers.

Math Notes encourage students to spend most of their time preparing to solve the problem. This pre-solution thinking is especially important as problems become more complex and less routine, ensuring that students break the problem down and see the big picture (i.e., what the problem is asking and what it looks like) before they try solving the problem.

How to Use the Notemaking Tool

Use Organizer 2-C, "Math Notes," on page 73.

Incorporate Math Notes into your classroom using the following steps:

1. Present students with a word problem that they must solve. Have students use Organizer 2-C, "Math Notes," to break down the parts of the problem in this sequence:
    *   In "The Facts" box, they identify the facts of the problem and determine what is missing.
    *   In "The Question" box, they isolate the main question that the problem is asking, and they search for hidden questions or assumptions.
    *   In "The Diagram" box, they visualize and draw the problem as they see it.
    *   In "The Steps" box, they determine what steps should be taken to solve the problem.
2. Challenge students to solve the problem by following the process in "The Steps" box on the organizer. They may use the back of the organizer to solve the problem.

3. Instruct students to check their work for accuracy (did I add, subtract, multiply, divide, etc., correctly?), reasonableness (does the answer make sense?), and appropriateness (does my solution answer the question?). (Make sure students know basic checking techniques like estimating, guessing and checking, and working backwards.)

4. Have students keep the problems and solutions in a special notebook or folder. This collection of problems serves as a reference guide for students: when students encounter difficult word problems, they can refer to this collection, look for any similar problems, and use them to help solve the new problem. Over time, students will begin to identify and categorize different types of word problems and, more importantly, be able to apply the most useful problem-solving process to each.

Helping the Struggling Notemaker

Often, students about to solve word problems leap before they look. To make matters worse, traditional problem-solving approaches often emphasize finding solutions over internalizing and understanding the problem. One of the most important ideas of Math Notes is that of slowing students down and engaging them in four powerful pre-solution thinking strategies. Modeling and practice sessions will play an important role in getting students out of the habit of impulsive problem-solving. Focusing one by one on the four strategies that make up Math Notes and moving progressively toward finding solutions can also help students focus their attention on getting prepared to solve the problem.

Name: _____

Math Notes

The Facts

What are the facts?

What is missing?

The Steps

What steps can we take to solve the problem?

The Question

What question(s) needs to be answered?

Are there any hidden questions that need to be answered?

The Diagram

How can we represent the problem visually?

Now use the back of this page to solve the problem.

Chapter Three

Eyes-On, Minds-On Reading

Chapter Overview: Advance Organizer

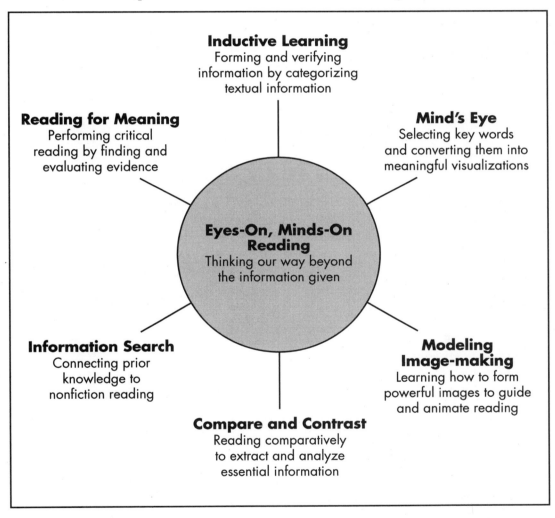

Inductive Learning
Forming and verifying information by categorizing textual information

Mind's Eye
Selecting key words and converting them into meaningful visualizations

Reading for Meaning
Performing critical reading by finding and evaluating evidence

Eyes-On, Minds-On Reading
Thinking our way beyond the information given

Information Search
Connecting prior knowledge to nonfiction reading

Modeling Image-making
Learning how to form powerful images to guide and animate reading

Compare and Contrast
Reading comparatively to extract and analyze essential information

> ## "Reading is the creation of ideas out of the invisible."
>
> Ann Lute
> High School English Teacher

Writers ask a lot of readers. They expect us to see the invisible. After all, the only items in our sight when we read are the white page and the black letters. The lions of the Savannah, the motivations of soldiers, the rhythms of the heart, and the structure of an argument all happen elsewhere—off the page. If we are to understand them we will have to supply them, create them out of the machinery of our minds.

Yet traditional reading programs have left the role of thinking about reading until after students have read the text. We now know that good readers think not only after reading, but also before, and especially during reading, whether five, nine, or ninety years old. Proficient readers do this naturally. Take this example:

> "Nearly all life in the rain forest begins, ends, and begins again on the shadowy forest floor. The floor is carpeted with a shallow layer of leaf litter; the few plants that grow there, such as ferns and broad-leafed plants, have large thin leaves that can absorb whatever sunlight reaches them." (Lyman, 1998)

When proficient readers read this passage, for instance, their minds show them the shadows at their feet, they hear the leaves crunch beneath them and feel the sunlight falling on the leaves. These *images* supply much of the meaning and most of the pleasure they find in reading. Now read this passage:

> "Richard loved to hear his grandfather tell about the war, how he ran away from his master and fought the rebel army." (Miller, 1997)

When proficient readers read a passage like this excerpt from the biography of the great African-American writer Richard Wright, their minds look for word clues like "war," "master," "rebel," and "army." Using these word clues as mind-activators, they connect the new reading to relevant prior knowledge to infer that Richard's grandfather was a slave who fought with the North during the Civil War.

Finally, read this example:

> "Occasionally, a great many meteors will flash across the sky in a spectacular celestial show known as a meteor shower. These atmospheric displays occur at regular intervals, when at the same time each year Earth passes through the dust from certain comets. As our planet moves through such a meteor storm, numerous shooting stars seem to fly out from a distant point in the sky." (Saffer, 1998)

In this type of passage, proficient readers notice that the text follows a pattern: Result (meteor shower) followed by the cause (passing through the tail of a comet). They then reverse the pattern to see that the Earth's passing through a comet's tail causes meteor showers to appear. This ability to *reason* while reading helps proficient readers focus on and work through difficult passages or areas of a text.

Thus, in order to move beyond the literal—in order to become eyes-on, minds-on readers capable of making inferences—proficient readers engage in four distinct forms of thinking:

1. They make connections between what they are reading and the relevant, objective knowledge (as with the excerpt from Richard Wright's biography).
2. They apply their reasoning skills to focus on patterns and clues in the text that can help them make inferences or predictions about the text (as with the passage on meteor showers).
3. They create images out of the author's words, pictures, feelings, and sounds that bring life and meaning to the text (as with the rain forest reading).
4. They are aware of their own reading processes as they read. They know when they understand a text and when the reading has become confusing or lifeless. In the case of the latter, proficient readers take one of the three actions above to improve their understanding (as you may have done with any or all three of the readings).

Expert readers perform most of these actions easily, fluently, and largely unconsciously, but school-age children need to be taught how to apply these thinking strategies explicitly. Students need modeling and practice—lots of practice—to become the proficient readers we long for them to be.

In this chapter, we will explore six strategies that foster the development of these essential skills:

Information Search, which helps students forge connections between what they already know and what they are reading.

Reading for Meaning, Inductive Learning, and **Compare and Contrast,** which help students become sensitive to patterns and reason their way to successful inferences and predictions.

Modeling Image-making and **Mind's Eye,** which help students use their imaginations to construct images and derive meaning and pleasure from what they read.

INFORMATION SEARCH

The Strategy in Action

Enda Anbey is preparing her students for a study of the American Revolution. On the chalkboard, she displays the beginnings of a concept map with the main subtopics to be addressed by the chapter, but she has translated these subtopics into questions:

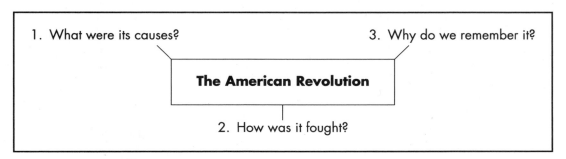

1. What were its causes?
3. Why do we remember it?

The American Revolution

2. How was it fought?

Information Search: first step—starting a concept map

Enda then breaks the class into groups, which will each focus on one of the three questions by brainstorming about it. Enda tells students that in brainstorming, they should rely not only on what they know about the question; students should also include what they think they know, what they believe, and how they feel about the question. Student groups create lists of their brainstorms, and Enda asks each group to share its ideas with the class. As students share their ideas, Enda records them on the board. Then Enda works with students to assess the information, placing a question mark next to whatever information students are unsure about or disagree over.

1. What were its causes?
   - Taxes.
   ? • They took our money.
   - We wanted independence.

3. Why do we remember it?
   - We became our own country.
   ? • Declaration of Independence

The American Revolution

2. How was it fought?
   - George Washington was the General
   ? • We wore red uniforms.
   ? • They wore red uniforms.
   - They used muskets.
   ? • What's a musket?

Information Search: second step—brainstorming

Students use this organizer to structure their reading by verifying information and by focusing on the areas of uncertainty to find answers. As they read, students use a set of reader's punctuation, which Enda has modeled with them:

- An exclamation point (!) identifies new information.
- A lightning bolt (⚡) identifies information that disagrees with information on the organizer.
- An asterisk (*) identifies information that agrees with information on the organizer.

After reading, students work together to build visual organizers that blend old, new, and corrected information. Some students create more elaborate webs, but Charlotte and Murphy, for example, create a comparison organizer that compares and contrasts American and British positions relevant to each of the three questions.

	Colonists	British
Cause	Taxes Independence	Wanted to keep America as a colony Tobacco
War	Fought from trenches George Washington - General Benedict Arnold - traitor Saratoga, Trenton - major victories	Fought in lines Lord Cornwallis General Burgoyne
Importance	We gained independence	Book didn't say We think it's important because they lost a big colony
Both		
Used muskets—an old-fashioned rifle "Pride was at stake" Was an important event for both England and America Lost a lot of soldiers		

Information Search: third step—building a visual organizer

Why the Strategy Is Beneficial

Information Search is built on the foundation of K-W-L (see Chapter One). While K-W-L provides a solid framework for developing students' informational reading skills, its basic structure can be strengthened to help students become deeper readers.

In response to the weaknesses in K-W-L, Silver and Strong (1994) have developed a variation on K-W-L known as Information Search to spur greater student engagement in the reading and learning process. Information Search maximizes the benefits of prior knowledge, active reading, elaboration, and constructive reflection by making three important alterations to K-W-L.

1. In K-W-L, the simple naming of a topic as a way to activate prior knowledge is sometimes not enough to stimulate students' memories. With Information Search, students are given the topic and its important subtopics rather than just the topic. This provides richer stimulus for activating prior knowledge and encourages students to delve deeper into their memory banks to access that knowledge.

2. In K-W-L, the questions students generate are sometimes too open, and may not be answered by reading. This may render the reading irrelevant to students' concerns, which can inhibit active reading. In Information Search, students mark the text for specific information using a set of meaningful symbols (!—new information, ⚡—information that disagrees with information on the organizer, *—information that agrees with information on the organizer). This element ensures that students' reading is both active and directed toward relevant information.

3. K-W-L does not allow students to process the text in sufficient depth to elaborate upon how their understanding has been changed or expanded by active reading. This weakness conflicts with research that shows elaborating upon emerging comprehension is essential to building deep and permanent understanding (Reder, 1980). Using Information Search, once students have processed the text, they must work together to construct a new organizer showing old, new, and corrected information. In this way, students not only determine what they have learned, as they do in K-W-L, but they must also elaborate on this information by synthesizing their prereading, reading, and post-reading activity into a complete picture of their understanding.

How to Use the Strategy

Use Organizers 3-A and 3-B on pages 83–84: "What We Know, Think We Know, Feel (Before Reading)" and "What We Now Know as a Result of Our Reading and Discussion."

Incorporate the Information Search strategy in your classroom using the following steps:

1. Select an appropriate reading.
2. Survey the reading and identify the important subtopics.
3. Have students generate what they know, think they know, and feel about each subtopic using Organizer 3-A, "What We Know, Think We Know, Feel (Before Reading)." (To refine and maximize input, this process is often done individually, in small groups, and then with the whole class.)
4. Help students use the subtopics and the results of their brainstorming to identify questions for research.
5. Provide the reading for students to conduct their research. Show them how to use reader's punctuation to actively search for information:
   - ! New information
   - ⚡ Information that disagrees with the information on the organizer
   - * Information that agrees with information on the organizer
6. Have students create a new concept map with the revised information using Organizer 3-B, "What We Now Know as a Result of Our Reading and Discussion."

Helping the Struggling Reader

As with K-W-L, students may encounter difficulties in brainstorming about what they already know, in generating questions for reading, and in the actual reading of the text. Thus, in helping struggling readers develop proficiency in using Information Search, you should use the same techniques as those described in the Helping the Struggling Reader section of K-W-L (pages 32–33):

- Use simple, obvious questions that help students tap into their knowledge base to generate what they already know.
- Use probing questions to help students find the questions they have.
- Use various techniques, such as modeling, read alouds, collaborative reading, and multiple inputs to help students engage in active, in-depth reading.

Name: _____

What We Know, Think We Know, Feel (Before Reading)

Subtopic/Question A	Subtopic/Question B

Topic

Subtopic/Question C	Subtopic/Question D

Name: _____

What We Now Know as a Result of Our Reading and Discussion

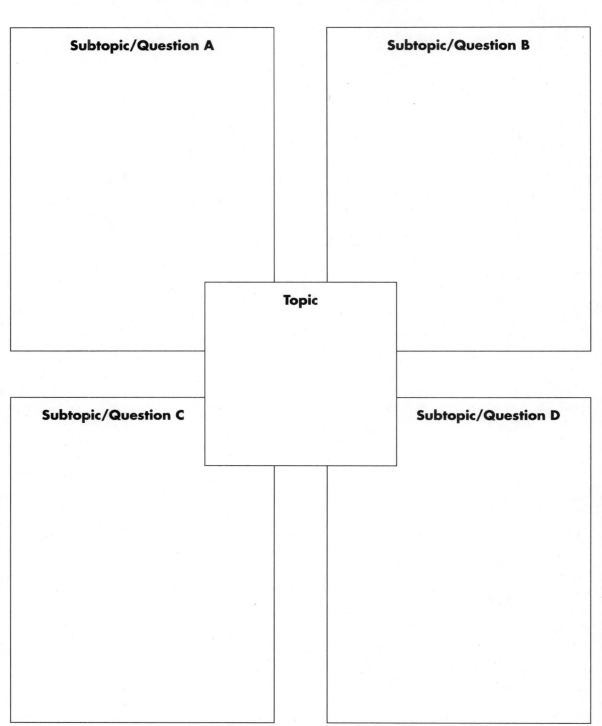

Subtopic/Question A

Subtopic/Question B

Topic

Subtopic/Question C

Subtopic/Question D

READING FOR MEANING

The Strategy in Action

Colin Goldberg's second graders are learning about healthy eating. Today, Colin is reading Mitchell Sharmat's *Gregory the Terrible Eater* aloud to his students. Behind him is an easel on which Colin has written three statements in a particular format. (See diagram.)

Both before and as Colin reads the book aloud, he asks students to think about the statements he has written. At key points in the reading, Colin stops and asks students if they notice anything in the story that might help them decide if the statements are true or false. If the students' information suggests that a statement is true, he writes it in the "Proof For" column. If the information suggests that a statement is false, he writes it in the "Proof Against" column. After completing the chart, Colin and his students discuss the reading and the statements to see how the reading has changed students' ideas about nutrition. In this way, Colin is helping his students develop the crucial skill of collecting evidence and using it to support or refute ideas.

Proof For		Proof Against
	Gregory is a healthy eater	
	Gregory eats what humans should eat	
	Gregory is eating the right foods for a goat	

Using the Reading for Meaning strategy to search for evidence

* * *

"Collecting and making good use of evidence," explains Kirsten Hardaway to her fifth graders," is one of the most important reading and research skills there is." Like Colin Goldberg, Kirsten also uses Reading for Meaning to promote evidence-based reading, but with a yearlong emphasis on building student independence. At the beginning of the year, Kirsten provides students with statements to use in analyzing a reading.

As the year progresses, Kirsten shifts responsibility for using the strategy to students. For some readings, Kirsten asks students to create their own statements and then to trade these statements with a partner. Each student uses his or her partner's statements to conduct the reading. Partners then meet to discuss each other's statements and, if necessary, to rewrite them so they are keyed to essential information.

To further build student independence, Kirsten shows students how to use the strategy to manage difficult readings. When students become confused by what they are reading, she explains that they can stop reading and instead focus on creating a statement that they believe tells what the passage is about. Students can then use this statement to check whether the reading supports their belief.

Why the Strategy Is Beneficial

Strategic reading is a goal in every classroom where reading takes place. But what exactly is meant by the term strategic when it comes to reading? Beth Ann Herrman (1992) in her work on strategic reasoning defines the application of strategic reasoning to reading and writing as the "complex thinking processes used before, during, and after reading and writing to construct meaningful interpretations of text and to create meaningful texts" (page 428). Central to Herrman's formulation is the idea that the strategic reader interacts with the text at three distinct points: before reading, during reading, and after reading.

Reading for Meaning (Silver, Hanson, Strong, & Schwartz, 1996) is adapted from Harold Herber's work with Reading and Reasoning Guides (1970) and is designed specifically to make students active participants in the three-part structure of strategic reading through three phases: pre-reading, active reading, and post-reading:

- In the pre-reading activity, students preview statements about the text prior to reading it, thus helping students to intuitively develop an image of the text's structure. Second, students are asked to decide whether each statement is true or false before reading, thereby activating the power of prior knowledge by asking students to use it to make predictions about the reading. As Tierney and Cunningham (1984) report, both of these pre-reading activities make reading significantly more manageable for students.
- In the active reading stage, students read with a purpose, searching for evidence to support or refute the statements.
- Post-reading activity is stimulated by asking students to look back at their statements and consider how their understanding has changed or evolved as a result of the reading.

How to Use the Strategy

Use Organizer 3-C, "Reading for Meaning," on page 88.

Incorporate the Reading for Meaning strategy into your classroom using the following steps:

1. Provide students with three to five statements keyed to major ideas in a reading. Have students copy the statements onto Organizer 3-C, "Reading for Meaning." Ask students whether they think the statements are true or false.
2. Instruct students to read the text, looking for evidence that corresponds to each statement and recording it on their organizer, either in the "Evidence For" or "Evidence Against" column.
3. After reading, ask students to meet with other students to discuss their evidence and to try to reach consensus for each statement.
4. Lead a discussion in which you survey positions and discuss the role of textual evidence in defending positions.

5. To extend the learning, you may want to challenge students to elaborate on their new knowledge or to use their new knowledge to create a summary or interpretation of the reading.

6. Teach students how to use the strategy independently by developing statements and using them to verify understanding.

Helping the Struggling Reader

The primary difficulty students experience during a Reading for Meaning lesson is finding and using appropriate evidence to support or refute the statements. Obviously, teacher modeling is essential. Beyond modeling, however, the following ideas will help students develop competence in evidence gathering:

1. Be literal at first. The first time you use Reading for Meaning with students, begin with literal statements that are explicitly addressed in the reading. Over time, you can make the statements more inferential, but by beginning with the literal, you can greatly boost students' confidence in their ability to track down evidence.

2. Encourage text-marking or text-posting. If the students are able to write directly on their readings, let them underline, highlight, and mark up the text to help them find relevant information. If they can't write on their text, then provide them with Post-It notes they can use to mark essential information. Or, teach them to use reader's punctuation like the following:

   + This supports a statement.

   – This refutes a statement.

   ? I think this is important but I'm not exactly sure how.

3. Practice using evidence in everyday activities. Get students accustomed to the idea of using evidence before they begin reading. For example, a third-grade teacher from Georgia began a class by saying, "The Atlanta Braves are a great baseball team." Then she asked students to provide evidence for or against this statement. Students' responses included: "They played in the World Series." "They have three Cy Young pitchers on the team." "They always win their division." In this way, students were able to see what it means to gather evidence before being asked to do it in conjunction with a text.

4. Use statement strips. Give students a sheet of strips containing facts about a topic (e.g., "Spiders eat insects that carry diseases"). Then provide students with a statement such as, "Spiders are helpful to humans." Ask students to cut up their strips and to determine whether the information supports or refutes your statement. Students can paste their strips onto an organizer or piece of posterboard divided into "Supports" and "Refutes" columns. This activity is a fun, hands-on way to get students to evaluate evidence.

Name: _____

Reading for Meaning

Proof For	Statement	Proof Against

INDUCTIVE LEARNING

The Strategy in Action

Teacher Maggie O'Hagan knows that when students make predictions about a text, their reading becomes an active search, an inquiry spurred by curiosity about whether they were right. This is why Inductive Learning is one of her favorite instructional strategies.

Currently, Maggie is using Inductive Learning as part of her unit on Colonial America. Using a reading on the way Colonial New Englanders lived, Maggie selects approximately 30 words and phrases from the reading that support the generalizations she expects students to make. For instance, one of the essential ideas in the reading is that Colonial New Englanders were very religious. To support this idea, Maggie selects the following words from the reading:

> sin
> minister
> Sabbath
> Bible
> faith
> prayer
> congregation

Once she has completed selecting key words for each big idea in the reading, Maggie gives them to students and asks them to analyze the words and then, in small groups, to group the words into categories based on common attributes. Once students have grouped the words, they must devise a descriptive label for each group that succinctly identifies the common relationship among the words.

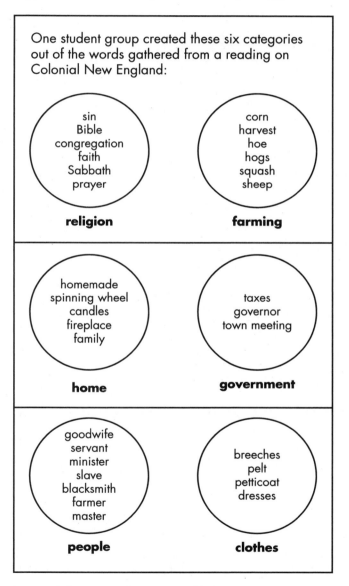

One student group created these six categories out of the words gathered from a reading on Colonial New England:

religion
sin
Bible
congregation
faith
Sabbath
prayer

farming
corn
harvest
hoe
hogs
squash
sheep

home
homemade
spinning wheel
candles
fireplace
family

government
taxes
governor
town meeting

people
goodwife
servant
minister
slave
blacksmith
farmer
master

clothes
breeches
pelt
petticoat
dresses

Words from a reading, grouped by category

Students then use their groupings to make three hypotheses about life in Colonial New England. Among the most common predictions Maggie hears from her students are:

"Life was hard."

"They were very religious."

"Farming was how they got food."

"They had simple clothes—not a lot of extras like jewelry."

"Family was very important."

Once students make their three hypotheses, they read the selection and use it to find out if they were correct or mistaken. Using a support-refute organizer, students jot down evidence from the selection that supports or refutes each hypothesis in the appropriate space.

Hypothesis	Support	Refute

Support-Refute Organizer

To move her students toward independence, Maggie explains to students that this process is especially helpful when a reading becomes difficult. By starting with the words that seem important and then using those words to build a meaning, the reader can work through the reading and develop a general understanding of its important ideas. This gives the student a reading framework he or she can use to "crack" the difficult text.

Why the Strategy Is Beneficial

Inductive Learning is based on a three-part process designed by Hilda Taba (1971). Taba found that if students were asked to enumerate and examine related items; group these items into meaningful categories and provide descriptive labels for each group; and make predictions based on those groups, they became better able to make generalizations and find big ideas in the content they were learning. By asking students to search for patterns, think flexibly about possible relationships, summarize these relationships through labeling, and use these self-created relationships to find meaning, Inductive Learning taps into students' natural potential for making inferences.

Four elements of Inductive Learning make it particularly powerful as a reading strategy:

1. It introduces students to the skills of identifying key words and phrases in a reading.
2. It asks students to form a conceptual framework by developing groups before they read.
3. It asks students to make predictions about what the reading will contain.
4. It asks students to search for relevant evidence.

How to Use the Strategy

Use Organizer 3-D, "Support/Refute," on page 93.

Incorporate the Inductive Learning strategy into your classroom, using the following steps:

1. Identify key words and phrases from the text and distribute them to students. (You can also work with students to enumerate words and phrases from the text.)
2. Model the process of grouping and labeling.
3. Have students form small groups to analyze the words and to explore the different ways information can be grouped.
4. Ask students to devise a descriptive label for each of their groups.
5. Have students use their labels and word groupings to make several predictions or hypotheses about the reading. Students should write their hypotheses in the appropriate space in Organizer 3-D, "Support/Refute."
6. Instruct students to read the text using Organizer 3-D to search for evidence that supports or refutes their hypotheses.
7. Ask students to reflect on the Inductive Learning process and lead a discussion on what they have learned from it.
8. Teach students how to use the process of identifying words, creating groups, and generating predictions as an independent reading strategy.

Helping the Struggling Reader

It may take some time before students become independent users of Inductive Learning. Help students master the strategy by modeling the different processes (generating, grouping and labeling, predicting, collecting evidence) and allowing time for students to practice it.

For students who are struggling while trying to group information from a text, you may want to use concrete objects such as fruits, vegetables, money, toys, etc., to help them develop grouping skills through hands-on grouping activities Also, you can help students gain confidence in their abilities to classify information by providing them with the labels and asking them to create groups accordingly.

Also, it is a good idea to talk with students about their reasons for grouping, for example:

- Is the reason for grouping categorical? Are the members of the group all examples of one thing (e.g., France, Chile, India, and Kenya are all countries)?
- Is the reason for grouping descriptive? Are the members of the group connected by similarities in shape, appearance, color, texture, material, etc. (e.g., cotton, feathers, pillows are all soft)?
- Is the reason for grouping based on a part-to-whole relationship? Are the members of the group all part of something larger (e.g., door, window, kitchen, living room are all parts of a house)?
- Is the reason for the grouping relational or inferential? Are items grouped according to an abstract quality shared by the whole group (e.g., rain, cloud, mild, and foggy all have to do with the weather)?
- Is the reason for the grouping mixed? Does it use some combination of the above? Or does it follow another pattern altogether?

In terms of trouble students may encounter in gathering relevant evidence to support and refute their hypotheses, refer to the "Helping the Struggling Reader" section in Reading for Meaning (page 87).

Name: _____

Support/Refute

Hypothesis	Support	Refute

COMPARE AND CONTRAST

The Strategy in Action

Amy Wheeler is teaching her second graders about spiders. When she began her unit, she found that most students think spiders are insects. Today, to help them overcome this misconception, Amy is going to show her class how to discriminate between two objects in order to make careful observations and draw thoughtful conclusions.

Amy begins by asking her students to think about cats and dogs. She asks them to think about what makes a dog a dog and what makes a cat a cat. "How do they look? What do they eat? What are some things they do?" she asks. She asks the class to use these three criteria to describe each animal separately. As students respond, she records their ideas on the board. Once each animal has been adequately described, Amy draws a Venn Diagram on the board. She labels one circle "cats" and the other "dogs" and uses the information from the description to fill in the diagram with her students. Then, Amy asks her students what characteristics both animals share and records student responses in the overlapping section of the diagram.

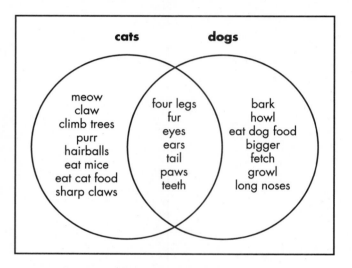

Venn Diagram used to compare and contrast

After Amy discusses this process of comparing and contrasting, she turns to the selected reading on spiders and insects. Before the reading, she hands out pieces of paper on which the students draw their own Venn Diagrams for similarities and differences. Once again, she asks students to first focus on what each looks like, eats, and does. She reads the text two times, asking her students to listen the first time without writing and then to write down their observations the second time as she reads more slowly. After the description phase, students use their Venn Diagrams to discriminate between spiders and insects by recording similarities and differences.

When the students are finished, Amy checks their comprehension of the readings and the effectiveness of their organizers by asking what makes a spider a spider, what makes an insect an insect, and what characteristics they both share. She lists student responses on the board and then asks students to decide if spiders and insects are more alike or more different. For a final activity, Amy asks her students to write a brief response to this question: "Would you rather be a spider or an insect? Why?"

Why the Strategy Is Beneficial

In 1990, Mullis, Owen, and Phillips published a report asserting that American students generally lack the skills needed to make sophisticated comparisons. According to Marzano (1992), this condition is exacerbated by the fact that educators across the country often see comparing and contrasting as skills that are too basic to refine and develop. Comparing and contrasting, however, are the foundations for serious thought as naturally engages students in the essential cognitive processes of classifying, analyzing, and using data appropriately. And, while comparison is natural to human thinking, it will only become a sophisticated, analytical tool if it is applied by students "consciously and rigorously" (Marzano, 1992, pg. 73).

As a reading strategy, Compare and Contrast gives students a powerful means of extracting essential information from a text or multiple texts, even if they lack background knowledge on the subject matter. Development of independent comparative thinking occurs in three progressive stages. In the first stage, students learn to describe topics in terms of their similarities and differences. In the second, they develop the ability to use similarities and differences in terms of given criteria such as function, location, size, shape, and components to differentiate between topics. In the third stage, students become able to formulate criteria themselves and to analyze topics according to specific similarities and differences that fit those criteria. In this third stage, students no longer need the teacher's help: they can read comparatively on their own by using the structure of the strategy to identify and extract the essential information from the reading or readings.

How to Use the Strategy

Use Compare and Contrast Organizers 3-E, 3-F, or 3-G (pages 98–100): "Three-Box Organizer," "Venn Diagram," or "Side-by-Side Diagram."

Incorporate the Compare and Contrast strategy into your classroom using the following steps:

1. Introduce the process of comparison by first comparing simple, everyday objects that students know already—cats and dogs, apples and oranges, winter and spring.
2. Select and distribute Compare and Contrast Organizer 3-E, 3-F, or 3-G. Choose two separate readings or a reading describing two different things that students will compare and contrast.
3. Establish the purpose for comparison by answering the question, "Why are we conducting a comparative reading?"
4. Provide students with criteria for analyzing the two items (e.g., "What do they eat? What do they look like? How do they behave?")
5. Have students use the criteria to describe each item separately.
6. Show students how to use Organizer 3-E, 3-F, or 3-G to differentiate between the two objects by recording similarities and differences.

7. Lead a discussion on one of the following topics:
    * Are the two more alike or more different?
    * What is the most important difference? What are the causes and effects of this difference?
    * What conclusions can you draw?
8. Move students toward independence in formulating criteria describing items and determining their similarities and differences.

Helping the Struggling Reader

For readers who are having difficulty reading comparatively, these interventions can prove helpful:

* Use notemaking as a complementary tool for comparison. Notemaking tools such as Graphic Organizers (see Chapter Two), text glossing, and reader's vocabulary (e.g., a "+" to indicate a similarity, a "−" to indicate a difference) can help students see critical relationships and make richer comparisons.
* For students who are having trouble analyzing the reading for similarities and differences, provide them with or show them how to create a Side-by-Side Diagram that will structure and focus their reading around similarities and differences. For example, using the Side-by-Side Diagram below, students will have an easier time extracting key information from their reading.

	Sedimentary	Metamorphic
Physical characteristics		
Examples of each		
How are they formed?		

Side-by-Side Diagram

Or, to further simplify the process, you might use a Comparison Matrix so that all students have to do is fill in "+" or "−" signs when analyzing topics in a reading or readings.

	Winter	Spring	Summer	Fall
Warm				
Hot				
Cold or cool				
Leaves fall				
Trees blossom				
Snow				
No school				

Comparison Matrix

Name: _____

Three-Box Organizer

Differences	Differences

Similarities

Venn Diagram

Name: _____

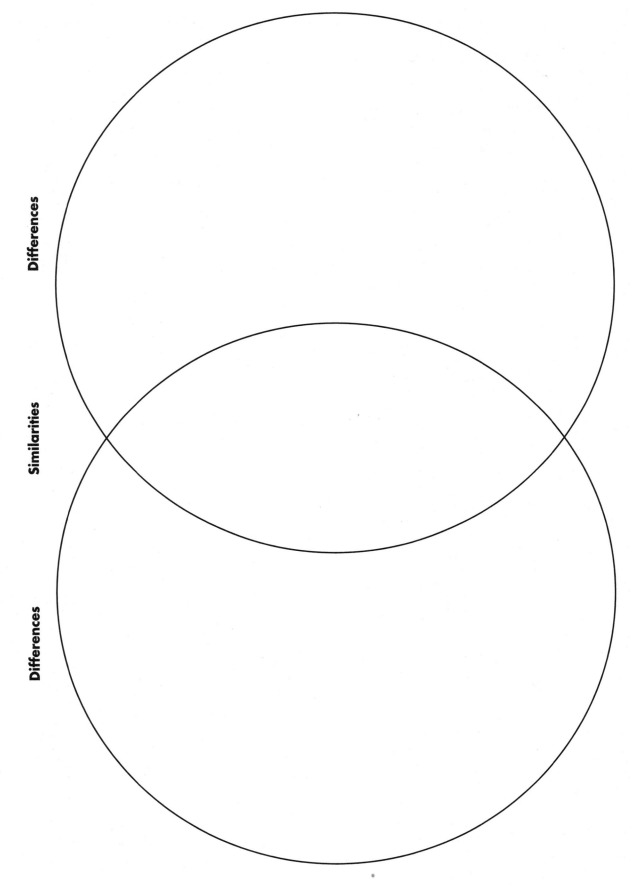

Differences

Similarities

Differences

Name: _____

Side-by-Side Diagram

Criteria for Comparison	1.	2.	Both

MODELING IMAGE-MAKING

The Strategy in Action

Teacher Jamie Gonzalez and a student, Marcie, sit facing each other. Marcie holds a book in her lap entitled *Outrageous Women of the Middle Ages* by Vicki Leon (1998). Jamie explains to students that today they will be exploring image-making in reading. She asks Marcie to begin reading the biographical sketch called "Aud, the Deep-Minded" aloud and slowly.

At the end of the first page, Jamie stops Marcie and says, "Tall. Muscular. Armor. These are words of power, words of strength. When you were describing how Aud grew up, I could really see her decked out in armor and holding an axe. She seemed very powerful, like a woman athlete today."

Later on Jamie stops Marcie again. "Converting to Christianity—I get a lot of images from that. When she converts to Christianity and becomes a wise woman I saw her and her people sitting around a fire. And Aud telling stories, and swaying while she talked. Aud the deep-minded—that's what I saw."

Near the end, Jamie stops Marcie yet again. "Being turned away by your own brother, that's very emotional. When you read about that, I felt so angry. She finally found her brother Helg after twenty years—and he wouldn't take her in. I could feel *my* body going tight and angry. I could see her throwing things around and storming out."

After they finish, the students break into pairs and take turns reading biographies of medieval women to each other and discussing the images that come to their minds. Later on, students work in their journals. Some draw pictures of the images they create. Others describe the images with words and speculate on the thoughts and feelings of the women they are studying. Still others used the Split Screen strategy (See Chapter One) to record both words and pictures from their learning. Jamie discusses the journal entries with students to help them see how they are doing as image makers.

Why the Strategy Is Beneficial

Nothing could be less traditional than the classroom above and, perhaps, nothing could be more essential. Books are not movies, and without moving pictures, sound effects, and music at their disposal, authors count on readers to supply the missing elements that make their words move, breathe, and give pleasure.

The failure of students to create images spontaneously may go a long way in explaining gaps in students' reading comprehension. Image-making is something proficient readers do automatically (Keene & Zimmermann, 1997) but that most readers need to be trained in doing (Pressley, 1977; Sadoski, 1985). Training students to form images is a relatively simple and short procedure: both Pressley (1976) and Gambrell and Bales (1986) report that elementary students, including poor readers, can learn how to form images while reading in a half an hour or less.

How to Use the Strategy

Incorporate Modeling Image-Making into your classroom using the following steps:

1. Model the process by reading a selection and stopping periodically to describe the images developed during the reading. (You may also involve students in modeling as readers and as tentative image makers.)
2. Have students form pairs to read texts (aloud or independently), form images, and discuss those images with their partners.
3. Expand students' image-making skills by having students:
   - Discuss their experiences and their images.
   - Hold conferences on the relationship between reading and image-making.
   - Do journal work on image-making in which students draw pictures, write descriptive paragraphs, describe their feelings, or use a word-image technique like Split Screen.

Helping the Struggling Reader

Nanci Bell (1991) makes four simple suggestions for helping students form images while reading:

1. Provide a purpose by explaining how and why image-making is an important reading skill.
2. Have the student select a picture from a book and ask the student to describe it. Since you can't see the picture, you should ask questions about the picture, which the student should answer as descriptively as possible. This activity helps build the connection between words and images.
3. Use a progressive structure so that students start by imaging words and gradually move on to imaging paragraphs and extended passages.
4. Use questions to help students focus on big ideas and important information (e.g., What does this passage seem to be saying? What does this paragraph describe?), especially for longer and more complex passages where students may have trouble focusing and finding images.

MIND'S EYE

The Strategy in Action

For the last few days, Horace Witherspoon has been helping his second graders to practice forming images of everyday objects. "What does it look like? What colors, shapes, textures do you see? Does it have a smell? Does it make any sounds? How does it feel—is it soft or rough or smooth?" he asked students as they closed their eyes and concentrated on things as simple as their books, their pets, and what they ate for breakfast.

Today, students are applying their image-making skills to reading as Horace teaches his students how to find the visual words while reading. Today's reading comes from Jacob Laurence's *Harriet and the Promised Land* (1993), a verse book about Harriet Tubman. Horace reads the first four pages of the book aloud:

> Harriet, Harriet,
> Born a slave,
> Work for your master
> From your cradle
> To your grave.
> Harriet, clean;
> Harriet, sweep.
> Harriet rock
> The child to sleep.

Horace then goes back and shows students how he picks words to help him create an image. "It's important," Horace tells his students, "not to underline too many words—just the ones that can help you see the picture in the words. So, for these lines, the words 'slave,' 'clean,' 'sleep,' and 'rock' all help me make a picture in my head. In my picture I see poor Harriet, working all the time. She cleans and sweeps and takes care of the children. She has no time for herself. She just works so much that it hurts. She wants to do other things like play hide-and-seek, read, and have fun. But she's a slave and she's only allowed to clean and sweep and take care of the children."

Horace repeats this process for the next few pages and then breaks students up into small groups to begin forming images of the text on their own by identifying a few key words and phrases. Students discuss their images with their groups and then Horace conducts a whole-class discussion on reading using images.

Later in the week, after students have had time to practice, Horace meets with each image-making group and asks them questions about how they are doing at finding key words and developing images: "What do you see? hear? feel? What do you think the author will talk about next? How will that change your image? What key words did you underline? How did you decide on those words?" Horace uses the information he learns from the conferences to determine which students need more practice and which students are ready to work independently.

Why the Strategy Is Beneficial

Mind's Eye is similar to Modeling Image-Making in that it teaches students how to form pictures in their minds in order to animate and deepen their reading, and that it draws from the same research base (Gambrell & Bales, 1986; Keene & Zimmermann, 1997; Pressley, 1976, 1977; Sadoski, 1985). However, there are several key differences between the strategies:

- Mind's Eye begins with non-textual image-making, giving students practice before they read.
- Mind's Eye places greater emphasis on the identification of key words and phrases than Modeling Image-Making.
- Mind's Eye makes conferences an essential part of the process of assessing and addressing students' needs and abilities.

The strategy has an interesting history. During the late 1970s teachers in the Escondido school district (1979) began to work with image-making, and something extraordinary occurred. They pretested students' reading abilities, applied image-making strategies, and then tested students again. In only six weeks, nearly all the students showed marked improvement in retention, comprehension, and vocabulary.

How to Use the Strategy

Incorporate the Mind's Eye strategy into your classroom using the following steps:

1. Ask students to practice thinking about and forming images of simple, well-known objects—a dog, an apple, a ringing bell, the sight and feel of a hamburger—anything that students know and can visualize. During these imaging sessions, use the following questions and prompts:
   - "What do you see?"
   - "What do you hear?"
   - "How do you feel?"
   Have students practice this image-making for brief periods of time over several days.
2. Show students how to pre-read a passage by identifying and underlining the key words necessary to create an image in the mind. Teach students to be economical in underlining words and to focus only on those words and phrases that contain the essential visual information.

3. Work with students individually and in small groups by asking them to read aloud and to discuss their methods for selecting words and forming images. During these conferences and group-imaging sessions, use the prompts below in addition to those in step 1:
    - "What do you think will come next?"
    - "How might your prediction change your image?"
    - "What words did you use to create your image?"
    - "How did you determine your key words?"
4. Use conferences to assess student competencies. Encourage proficient image-makers to work independently. Provide additional assistance to struggling students.

Helping the Struggling Reader

To help students form images, refer to Nanci Bell's (1991) suggestions for the Modeling Image-Making strategy on page 102.

Chapter Four

A Question Is a Quest

Chapter Overview: Advance Organizer

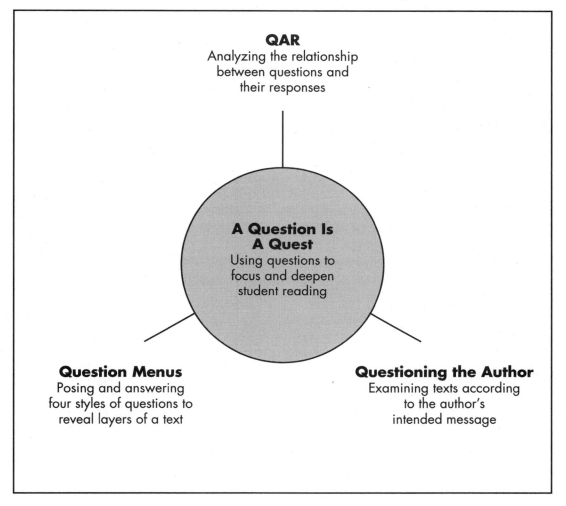

QAR
Analyzing the relationship between questions and their responses

A Question Is A Quest
Using questions to focus and deepen student reading

Question Menus
Posing and answering four styles of questions to reveal layers of a text

Questioning the Author
Examining texts according to the author's intended message

> *"Try to learn to love the questions."*
>
> Ranier Maria Rilke
> 20th Century German Poet

Where Questions and Answers Come From

In the beginning, a person has an experience: a child reads a book; a woman ruffles the back of her dog's head every day after work. Then, something happens: the child becomes confused by the reading; the dog doesn't greet the woman for his customary pet. That's when a question blossoms: What is the author saying? Is there something wrong with Spot? But this is only the beginning. The questions we form lead us into a search for answers. The child may reread the confusing passage to see what caused the confusion. The woman may begin to speculate about her dog's health and call the vet. Along the way and as this process progresses, we begin to develop answers to our questions: the book is using ideas that are new to me; Spot is sick. As we begin to solidify our answers by restating them to ourselves or talking to other people or writing in our journals, something remarkable happens: there is a response. For the reading child, the next chapter of the book clarifies the new ideas. The vet tells the woman the dog is fine.

The Questioning Cycle

What all this means is that questions are inherently incomplete. They live and thrive as part of a cycle that includes:

- Experiencing.
- Questioning.
- Answering.
- Response.

Cut any part or "gear" of the cycle off from the others and the "gears" do not make contact with one another. They are left spinning in space, alone, incomplete. The process breaks down. Teaching students that questions and answers

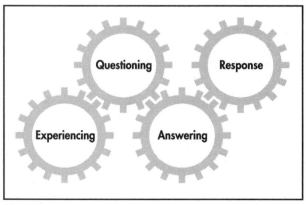

Parts or "gears" of the questioning cycle

are cyclical is essential if we want students to do more than simply answer questions. If we are to develop quality thinkers and quality readers, we must teach students how to formulate their own questions, develop their own strategies for seeking answers, seek the responses of others, and begin the cycle over again with a new set of questions.

This view of questions differs sharply from traditional perspectives. In the more standard view, questions belonged to teachers and were asked *after* the reading experience was over. Students were not taught how to use their reading experiences to create questions before, during, and after reading. They were not guided in seeking answers or encouraged to use others' responses as spurs to seek further questions or deeper answers. Teachers asked the questions and students spooned up the answers.

In the new view, the teacher models the entire question cycle for the students. She helps students to find their own questions to guide and clarify the meanings of texts. She carefully models how to search for and construct answers. She provides and encourages students to provide positive and constructive responses to other students' questions, and she teaches students to use these responses as tools to create further questions and deeper answers.

This chapter presents three strategies teachers can implement to help their students use questions, answers, and responses to promote deeper readings of nonfiction texts.

- **QAR** shows students how to distinguish between three kinds of commonly asked questions and how to use these distinctions to find the answers they need.
- **Questioning the Author** is a strategy designed to help students overcome the difficulties of nonfiction reading through a unique combination of questioning, modeling, and response.
- **Question Menus** teach students how to pose and answer four styles of questions and how to discover the kinds of questions and answers that are most meaningful to them.

QAR

The Strategy in Action

Alan Liu is teaching his fourth graders how to use the Internet. Today the class is going to read about Web pages in Asha Kalbag's *World Wide Web for Beginners* (1997).

Before reading, Alan holds a group review session in which students practice asking and answering each of the three types of question-answer-relationships (QARs): "right there" QARs, which are answered simply by finding and restating information from the reading; "think and search" QARs, which are answered by pulling together different pieces of information from the reading and synthesizing them; and "on my own" QARs, which are answered by tapping into personal knowledge and experience. During the group review session, Alan walks around the room to make sure students understand the three types of QARs.

Alan then pulls the class back together, has students read the passage on Web pages, and begins asking students questions. Before students answer the question, they must identify the QAR.

Alan: Jeff, what is a multimedia Web page?

Jeff: Let's see. That question is a "right there" question because the answer is right here at the top. A multimedia Web page has two or more methods of presenting information combined on the same page.

Alan: Great, Jeff. You're right, that was a "right there" question. Here's another question. This one's for Heather. Heather, what are the different ways Web pages present information?

Heather: Okay. That's a "think and search" question. The answer's not just in one place. To get an answer I need to kind of put the whole thing together.

Alan: Excellent! So what's the answer?

Heather: Well there's video and animation, music and sound, pictures, and just plain words.

Alan: You're right again. Now, Sam, how do you move around on a Web page so you can see all the great things that are on it?

Sam: We didn't read about that, so that means it's an "on my own" question because on my own questions aren't answered by the reading; they come from what you know.

Alan: Absolutely correct. The answers to "on my own" questions come from personal knowledge and experience. And do you know the answer, Sam?

Sam: Yeah. You move around on the screen by clicking on those little arrows on the corners of the page.

Alan: Good. Does everyone remember the movement arrows from the computer lab?

After asking a few more questions, Alan lets students ask each other questions about the reading on browsing the Web.

Why the Strategy Is Beneficial

In her research on questioning, Raphael (1982) found that students rarely receive training in how to analyze and answer the questions that are asked of them. In order to fill this gap, she developed the strategy known as QAR (Question-Answer-Relationships), relying on the work of Pearson and Johnson (1978), who describe three basic types of responses to questions based on reading:

1. Text-explicit responses come directly from the text. To generate a text-explicit response, the student determines what missing piece of information a question is asking him or her to find and then finds it in the text.
2. Text-implicit responses are constructed by the reader through a process of synthesizing information from the text. The student may need to piece together multiple bits of information in order to generate the answers.
3. Script-implicit responses are generated outside the text, out of the reader's experience and personal knowledge base. These questions require the student to call on what he or she knows and has experienced to develop an effective answer.

Essential to Raphael's strategy is training students how to identify the way different questions call for different types of responses. To make the strategy student friendly, Raphael calls the three response types "right there" (text explicit), "think and search" (text implicit), and "on my own" (script implicit).

Research on the strategy's effectiveness has shown that students who are familiar with the strategy are better able to generate quality answers to questions about their reading. Three studies (Raphael & McKinney, 1983; Raphael & Pearson, 1982; Raphael, Wonnacott, & Pearson, 1983) verify that the strategy has had successful results with students from fourth through eighth grade.

How to Use the Strategy

Use Organizer 4-A, "QAR: Question-Answer-Relationships," on page 114.

Incorporate the QAR strategy into your classroom using the following steps:

1. Explain and model the three types of QARs.
2. Create a variety of QAR questions keyed to a specific reading and write them in the "Question" column of Organizer 4-A, "QAR: Question-Answer-Relationships." Distribute the organizer to students.
3. Have students read the passage and use the text to identify the types of QARs and then to answer the question, using the appropriate spaces in Organizer 4-A.
4. Ask students to reflect on the process of answering each type of QAR.
5. Gradually move students toward independence by having them read passages and generate their own QARs.

Helping the Struggling Reader

The primary difficulty associated with QAR is that some students have trouble seeing the relationship between questions and the answers they ask readers to generate. Raphael (1982) makes four suggestions for helping students develop the analytical skills needed to make the connection between questions and their answers.

- Make sure that students, especially in the early phases, but also in the later phases, get immediate feedback so that their misconceptions do not solidify.
- Use a progressive reading structure so that students practice with short and simple texts and gradually move to longer and more complex ones.
- Make the question-answer relationships as explicit as possible at the beginning and use a majority of right-there questions so that the students become more confident in their abilities.
- Allow students to work in groups as they learn to identify question-answer relationships and construct responses. Over time, students will develop the skills needed to work independently.

Name: _____

QAR: Question-Answer-Relationships

Directions: _____

_____

Question	Answer	Type of QAR		
		Right There	Think and Search	On My Own

QUESTIONING THE AUTHOR

The Strategy in Action

George Billows has started a unit on ancient civilizations and is about to have his students read a passage about the importance of rivers in the formation of a civilization. He hands out copies of the reading to each of his students and asks them to follow along as he reads aloud.

George: Today we're going to try something a little different. Instead of reading this passage on your own, we're going to read it aloud together. As we read, I want you to think about what the author of this passage is trying to tell us. I'm going to be stopping during the reading to ask some questions, okay? Here we go.

George then begins the reading, stopping after certain sentences to spark discussion and to help students construct the meaning of the text by focusing on what the author is trying to say.

George: So what is the author trying to tell us here?

David: He says that when they plow the ground the soil gets looser and the rain washes it away.

George: David says that plowed soil gets washed away by the rain. Is the author clear about this? Does he say why this happens? Tanisha?

Tanisha: It says that plowing vertically makes the soil get washed away.

George: Tanisha has hit on a key word here, "vertically." Does anyone know what that means? Karen?

Karen: I think it means going up, you know, like a flagpole.

George: That's right. It means in an up and down direction. Now, where is the author trying to hint that people plow up and down? Try looking back a couple of sentences. What does the author mention? Joshua?

Joshua: He says that the mountains are a good place to defend against enemies because they're hard to climb but that they're not good for farming because the soil gets washed away.

George: So what Joshua is saying is that although the mountains are a great natural defense against enemies, trying to grow food on them is rather difficult. How does this connect to what the author has already told us?

Tanisha: I guess when they plowed up and down the mountain the rain would come and wash the soil away.

Lea: And so they couldn't grow crops.

George:	Excellent thinking, Tanisha and Lea. So then what would make it easier to plow the soil and grow crops? Chris?
Chris:	If the ground was flat then the soil couldn't wash away anywhere.
George:	And does the author suggest where the ground is flat enough so that plowed soil won't wash away with the rain?
Chris:	A river valley?
George:	Exactly. Now the author of this passage could have just said that in a river valley the land is flat and that this keeps the soil in one place when it rains, but authors don't always write so directly. And even when they do write that clearly, sometimes they assume that readers will question what they mean and piece together what they are trying to say like we just did. Let's read on and find out just how important farming was to ancient civilizations.

George continues to read and question his students until they have finished the passage. After reading, the class holds a discussion on the author's main points in the passage, and students who are confused clarify their understanding by asking questions.

Why the Strategy Is Beneficial

In the late 1980s, a number of researchers (Just & Carpenter, 1987; Perfetti, 1985) set out to identify the specific factors that cause difficulty for readers. Not surprisingly, these researchers found that readers had problems understanding the texts when they did not know the meaning of key words, lacked knowledge of the concepts contained in the reading, or were unable to locate and extract information. What researchers also found out is that comprehension is thwarted by texts themselves, for instance, when they make unclear references, are saturated with concepts, fail to establish a context for the content, or weakly link related information. More to the point for young readers of nonfiction, Beck, McKeown, and Gromroll (1989) found that much of the writing that appears in social studies textbooks lacks clear content goals, builds off background knowledge students don't have, and fails to provide in-depth explanations of complex topics.

Yet as murky as much textbook prose is, the prevailing attitude in schools is that nonfiction writing is above criticism. In response to this attitude, Questioning the Author (Beck, McKeown, Hamilton, & Kucan, 1997) is designed to help students actively construct meaning by focusing on the idea that a text is written by a person whose meanings and methods of presenting information must constantly be questioned. In order to help students reach this goal, Questioning the Author relies on four basic assumptions:

- Authors are human beings. They can be wrong. They can write poorly or unclearly.
- Reading is an active and segmented process. During their reading, readers wrestle with words and ideas by reading relatively short segments of text, questioning, constructing meaning, and then moving on to another relatively short portion of text.
- Wrestling with ideas requires talking as well as thinking. Collaboration, interaction, and idea "piggy-backing" are all part of constructing meaning and, therefore, are all part of the Questioning the Author process.
- The teacher, like the student, is also engaged in constructing meaning and must help students build understanding. To do this, the teacher uses *queries,* which differ from questions in that they:
  - Focus on helping students wrestle with ideas rather than assessing comprehension after reading.
  - Spur student interaction and discussion about the author's meaning rather than individual responses and teacher-to-student interaction.
  - Are used during the reading process rather than after it.

Beck and her associates suggest that teachers use initiating queries such as "What is the author trying to say here?" to get the author's ideas out in the open, then use follow-up queries like "How does that compare with what the author said before?" or "Does the author explain why this happens?" to focus thinking and discussion. Once the reading is complete, students reflect on the meaning of the text and on the Question the Author process so that they can see how the ideas of authorship and questioning are intimately related to reading. Over time, students can use these ideas to become independent and critical interrogators of the texts they read.

How to Use the Strategy

Incorporate the Questioning the Author strategy into your classroom using the following steps:

1. Begin by explaining that authors are not always clear and that sometimes what the author means is difficult to understand.
2. Direct students to begin reading a selected text. At key points in the reading, open a discussion with initiating queries, such as "What is the author trying to tell us here?" or "What is the author's intended message?"
3. To enable students to delve more deeply into a text's meaning, ask follow-up queries, such as "What does the author mean by that?"; "How does this connect or compare with what the author said before?"; and "Does the author explain why this happens?"
4. Have students discuss and reflect on the meaning of the text and on the Questioning the Author process.

Helping the Struggling Reader

Struggling readers as well as more competent readers may have difficulty comprehending the new idea that texts themselves may be unclear. This issue can be examined quite deeply through this simple activity:

1. Have students gather in groups of two or three, and instruct each member of the group to write a short piece (a summary, an essay, a reaction).
2. Direct students to exchange their writing within their groups. Each group member should try to summarize what the other person is trying to say in his or her piece.
3. After students have generated ideas, ask them to share their ideas with the class as you record them.
4. Then, ask the original student authors whether they agree or disagree with the ideas of their peers. When disagreements come up in the discussion, you can introduce the idea that, sometimes, authors and readers see things differently. Be sure to explain to students that this disagreement is natural and productive.

Other methods for helping students work through unclear passages include:

- Teaching students to stop regularly and write or draw a picture that explains what they believe the author is trying to say.
- Reminding students that every author is trying to answer a question or a set of questions and that part of reading is asking oneself, "What question is the author trying to answer?"

QUESTION MENUS

The Strategy in Action

To fourth-grade teacher Emily Sheffield, it is important that her students understand that reading is a multilayered process. In New York where Emily teaches, the new state standards have identified four essential kinds of reading: reading for information and understanding; for critical analysis and evaluation; for literary response and expression; and for social interaction. To Emily, this statewide reappraisal of reading is very exciting because it reflects what Emily has been doing for years in her classroom.

Among Emily's favorite strategies for engaging students in all four kinds of reading is the Question Menu. Currently, she is using Question Menus to help her students develop a deeper understanding of current events. Using an article called "Kosovo's Sorrow" from *Time for Kids*, Emily has designed four different questions for students to answer in processing the article. Emily places these questions in quadrants.

Information and Understanding (Task 1) What three events were the most significant in the history of the Kosovo crisis? Rank them in order.	**Social Interaction** (Task 4) What would you say to someone your own age who was suffering? Write a brief letter to a child in one of the refugee camps. Make sure that your letter lets the child know that you have heard his or her story.
Critical Analysis and Evaluation (Task 2) According to the article, why is peace so difficult to maintain in this region?	**Literary Response and Expression** (Task 3) Which image from the stories of the refugees stands out in your mind? Draw a picture or write a cinquain about it.

| *Question Menu*

After students have read the article, they review the four questions with Emily and then complete them in the given order. Students continually refer back to the article to check their understanding and to make sure they have the knowledge needed to answer each question. With each question, students add a new layer to their comprehension until they have a complete picture of the article's content. And not only have students been challenged to engage in different kinds of reading, but Emily now has a comprehensive set of assessment information that tells her where students need to further develop their thinking and reading skills.

Why the Strategy Is Beneficial

Nearly all research on reading agrees that a text operates on several levels simultaneously and that proficient readers know how to manage this "textual layering." For example, some portions of a text may be literal, with the meaning right at the surface (e.g., "The African elephant is approaching extinction"); other parts of a text may need to be pieced together or inferred (e.g., the complex cause-effect relationships involved in elephant extinction); other portions of a text might focus on imagery or on speculative thinking (e.g., what might happen ecologically if the elephant is driven to extinction); while still others might derive their power by appealing to the personal and emotional aspects of their content (e.g., urging everyone to help elephants survive by eliciting sympathy for their plight).

A Question Menu is designed to help students manage this textual layering by developing their abilities to think practically, logically, creatively, and personally about the texts they read. The strategy is based on the long and rich history of research on personality type beginning in 1921 with Carl Jung's groundbreaking *Theory of Psychological Types.* Jung studied differences in the way humans perceived the world (sensation vs. intuition) and the way they made decisions (objective thinking vs. personal feelings). What Jung found is that our preferences for sensing, intuition, thinking, and feeling develop into personality types.

The most famous application of Jung's theory came in 1962 when Isabel Myers developed the Myers-Briggs Type Indicator, a popular and renowned instrument for identifying personality type. Since Myers, a number of researchers (Butler, 1984; McCarthy, 1982; Silver & Hanson, 1998) have sought to understand how personality types play out in learning and in the education of students.

According to the Silver-Hanson learning style model, there are four basic learning styles:

Mastery	**Interpersonal**
The *Mastery style learner* absorbs information concretely; processes information sequentially, in a step-by-step manner; and judges the value of learning in terms of its clarity and practicality.	The *Interpersonal style learner,* like the Mastery learner, focuses on concrete, palpable information; prefers to learn socially; and judges learning in terms of its potential use in helping others and its personal relevance.
THE FOUR LEARNING STYLES	
Understanding	**Self-Expressive**
The *Understanding style learner* focuses more on ideas and abstractions; learns through a process of questioning, reasoning, and testing; and evaluates learning by standards of logic and the use of evidence.	The *Self-Expressive style learner* looks for images implied in learning; uses feelings and emotions to construct new ideas and products; and judges the learning process according to its originality, aesthetics, and capacity to surprise or delight.

| *Basic learning styles*

The types of thinking associated with each learning style can be engaged through different types of questions and activities (Strong, Hanson, & Silver, 1995):

Mastery questions ask students to:

Focus on recalling facts:
- Who was involved?
- Where did it take place?
- When did it occur?
- What happened?
- How did it occur?

Supply information based on observation:
- What did you observe?
- What is wrong with this? How would you correct it?
- Can you describe the data?

Establish procedures or sequences:
- What are the steps?
- How would you go about doing this?
- What comes first? Next?
- What is the correct order for this?

Interpersonal questions ask students to:

Empathize and describe feelings:
- How would you feel if _____ happened to you?
- How do you think _____ felt?
- Can you describe your feelings?

Value and appreciate:
- Why is _____ important to you?
- What's the value of _____?
- What decision would you make?

Explore human-interest problems:
- How would you advise or console _____?
- What is the issue facing _____? What would you do about it?
- How would you help each side come to agreement?

Understanding questions ask students to:

Focus on making connections:
- What are the important similarities and differences?
- What is the cause?
- What are the effects?
- How are the parts connected?

Make inferences and interpret:
- Yes, but why?
- How would you explain _____?
- Can you prove it?
- What can you conclude?
- What evidence do you have to support your position?

Focus on underlying meanings:
- What are the hidden assumptions?
- What does this prove?
- What have you discovered?

Self-Expressive questions ask students to:

Rethink their ideas:
- What comes to mind when you think of _____?
- How is _____ like _____?

Develop images, hypotheses, and predictions:
- What would happen if _____?
- Can you imagine _____? What would it look like? What would it be like?

Focus on alternatives and original solutions:
- How many possible ways can you _____?
- What is another way to do this?
- Is there a better way to design a _____?

Think metaphorically and creatively:
- How is _____ like _____?
- Can you create a poem, icon, or skit that represents this?

Question stem menu for all four learning styles

By using the Question Menus, teachers will teach students how to manage content and how to explore a reading deeply through a series of questions that emphasize facts and details (Mastery); logic and critical thinking (Understanding); creativity and expression (Self-Expressive); and personal and social relevance (Interpersonal). And not only is this diversification necessary to developing complete readers, it is also essential to building motivation in the classroom. As Hanson, Dewing, Silver, and Strong (1991) discovered in their research on 2,000 students at all grade levels, when the learning styles of some learners are routinely ignored, those learners tend to disengage from or feel threatened by the material they are learning. Question Menus provide a diverse structure for reading instruction and assessment that allows teachers to reach all students.

How to Use the Strategy

Use Organizer 4-B, "Question Menu," on page 124.

Incorporate Question Menus into your classroom using the following steps:

1. Select an appropriate text.
2. Using the Question Stem Menu on the previous page, establish one question in each style based on the reading. Write each question, or have students write each in the correct space in Organizer 4-B, "Question Menu." (You also may create multiple questions for each style and allow students to choose.)
3. Have students review the questions before reading.
4. Ask students to read and collect the information needed to generate a response for each question.
5. Allow students to meet with other students to discuss their responses.
6. Give students time to reflect on the styles of the questions and their personal preferences for each.
7. As students become competent, foster independence by encouraging them to ask their own style-based questions as a way to expose the multiple layers of a reading.

Helping the Struggling Reader

Below are five suggestions to help struggling students overcome the difficulty they may have in understanding the difference between the four types of questions.

1. Allow students to assess their own learning using the Hanson-Silver Learning Preference Inventory (1991), a multiple-choice instrument that assesses students' styles and shows teachers how to motivate each learner. (Refer to the last page of this book for more information.)
2. Introduce children's literature that deals with learning styles into your classroom. For example, *The Most Amazing Treehouse Ever* (Moses, 1997), *Bobby's Biking Lesson* (Robinson & Moses, 1997), and *Sam's Soccer Problem* (Robinson, 1997) are three picture books containing stories and activities that teach students about learning styles. (Refer to the last page of this book for more information.)

3. Directly teach students about learning styles. To make styles easier to understand, use simpler names for each style, such as "remembering" for the Mastery style, "reasoning" for Understanding, "creating" for Self-Expressive, and "relating" for Interpersonal. To make styles especially memorable, use visual icons to represent each (for instance, a check mark for Mastery, a question mark for Understanding, a painter's palette for Self-Expressive, and a heart for Interpersonal).

4. Introduce students to the four types of questions by modeling them in conjunction with a reading. Explain to students how each type of question allows the reader to see more deeply into the text. After modeling and practice, have students analyze the questions you provide rather than telling them what style each represents. Eventually, let students practice generating their own style-based questions.

5. Finally, regular use of four-style questioning in all content areas is not only a good way to get students used to style but is also important in developing balanced and adaptable learners who can explore content deeply. Below is a fifth-grade teacher's Question Menu for the first chapter of Collier and Collier's *My Brother Sam Is Dead.*

Mastery Comprehension	**Interpersonal Comprehension**
What is happening in the story? Who are the characters and what are their traits?	Which character do you relate to the most? The father, Sam, or Tim? Whom do you agree with, Sam or his father?
Understanding Comprehension	**Self-Expressive Comprehension**
What is the meaning of the story? Why are the characters arguing?	What do you imagine Tim is thinking during this argument? How is a colony like a child?

Question Menu for a reading

Name: _____

Question Menu

Directions: _____
_____

Mastery	**Interpersonal**
Understanding	**Self-Expressive**

Chapter Five

Write to Read

Chapter Overview: Advance Organizer

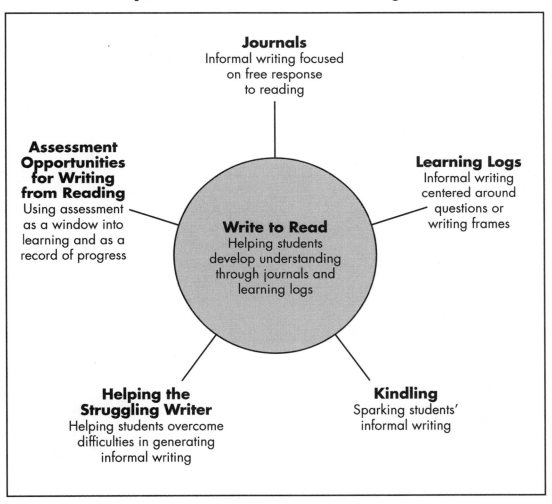

Journals
Informal writing focused on free response to reading

Assessment Opportunities for Writing from Reading
Using assessment as a window into learning and as a record of progress

Write to Read
Helping students develop understanding through journals and learning logs

Learning Logs
Informal writing centered around questions or writing frames

Helping the Struggling Writer
Helping students overcome difficulties in generating informal writing

Kindling
Sparking students' informal writing

> *"Language permits us to see. Without the word we are all blind."*
>
> Carlos Fuentes
> 20th Century Mexican Writer

People write for many reasons: to retell what they are reading and make sure they understand it; to note what's important and what's not; to connect what they are reading to their own knowledge and experience; to go beyond the information given to form predictions and images; and to raise questions for themselves and the author. We ask students to write before, during, and after reading in order to develop all the skills discussed in the previous chapters.

James Boyd White, the great scholar of law and literature, once declared, "Reading is an engagement of the mind that changes the mind." (1984, page x) We might say the same thing about writing. Writing is a primary tool for thinking and changing our thoughts about what we read and what we learn. Without the written word—the words readers write themselves—readers are blind. Therefore, a good rule of thumb for all teachers of reading is the old Latin proverb: "Never a day without a line."

However, there is another—and potentially deeper—reason for not letting a day go by without asking students to think and write about their reading: good writers tend to be good readers and good readers tend to be good writers. As the research indicates (Tierney & Shanahan, 1991; Vacca & Vacca, 1998), the more students write, the better they become at both reading and writing.

Yet, despite the many and good reasons for asking students to write regularly about their reading, many teachers express frustration at the low quality of student writing in journals and learning logs. Many students see maintaining these tools as a mindless and meaningless chore. Why does this happen?

We can think of informal writing in response to reading as a skill reminiscent of the questioning skills we explored in the previous chapter. Writing, like questioning, tends to:

- Emerge from experience.
- Improve with modeling and guided practice.
- Flourish when responded to in a positive and thoughtful manner and when used to provoke both more reading and more writing.

Writing from reading needs to be carefully introduced and cultivated in the classroom. This chapter presents several strategies and tools to help students gain expertise in the kind of writing that will help them become better readers:

- **Journals** are tools in which students freely record personal thoughts about what they have read.
- **Learning Logs** hold entries by students made in response to predetermined questions.
- **Kindling** is a questioning strategy used to spark students' interest and involvement in the writing process.
- **Helping the Struggling Writer** offers practical help for specific difficulties students experience in writing from reading.
- **Assessment Opportunities for Writing from Reading** shows teachers how to evaluate students' writing both by looking into their thinking and by paying attention to progress over time.

JOURNALS

In helping students use writing as a means for understanding texts, teachers can make use of two separate tools: Journals and Learning Logs. Both focus on the use of informal writing (spontaneous writing with little concern for writing conventions), and both frequently take place in a special composition book or separate section of a student's overall notebook; however, there are important distinctions between them.

- Journals tend to focus on students' free and open responses to what they read.
- Learning Logs are usually used to record students' thoughts about learning as directed by a teacher's question or through the use of a menu of questions from which the student chooses.

Selecting and developing writing assignments for nonfiction readers is a key skill in the teaching of reading. However, the good news in this respect is that there are many more ways to do this job well than there are to do it poorly. Once teachers build into their teaching practices the habits of modeling, rehearsing, and responding to student writing, the profusion of approaches is staggering. The following examples introduce two teachers, who will present and discuss excerpts from their students' journals.

Response Journal

Michele Chang
Fourth-Grade Teacher

"We do many kinds of writing in our classroom, but Response Journals play a regular and important role in everything we do. Three times a week I ask my students to write a response or a reaction to something we've read. I'm looking for their thoughts and feelings as they occur to them. I want their connections, not mine. In the beginning, the work with Response Journals is very hard. I see an awful lot of 'I liked it,' and 'It was nice.' But by keeping my own journal and sharing it with the kids and bringing in excerpts from scientists' and artists' and authors' journals, I see the kids' writing really improve. They get deeper. What I really like about David's entry is the way he saw the plight of the farmers and ranchers. The author didn't mention that at all. That's all David!"

David Garbiner

Response to editorial on destruction of rain forests

I enjoyed the editorial on what's happening to the rain forests. Well "enjoy" isn't quite right, but I liked reading it. I especially liked the way the author described the trees as "breathing for us." But the article made me worry too. If we do stop the farmers and ranchers who are burning the rain forests, who will feed their children?

Student's Response Journal

Dialogue Journals

Jerry Longman
Third-Grade Teacher

"We've been using Dialogue Journals for three years now. I simply ask the students as they read, or afterward, to write some quotes from what they're reading on the left side of the page and to write their thoughts and ideas on the right. I tell the kids I want them to catch themselves thinking. It's like playing tag with your mind. By the end of they year most of the projects my students do come directly out of these Dialogue Journals. But I don't use them all of the time. I'll work with them for a month or so, then put them away. Then I'll bring them back a month or two later. That way they don't become routine. What I like about Terri's journal is all these questions. That's a real pattern with Terri. Always questions, and good questions too. Look how she asks questions about how the author gets information for these books. That's something I like to see."

Terri Fine Third Grade	
Journal entry on the Magic School Bus and the Electric Field Trip	
The Electric Field Trip	**Me**
"It would take more than a million atoms to stretch across the width of one human hair." →	How can they be that small? How do scientists see them?
"But sometimes electrons get pulled away. They leave one atom and jump to the next." →	Where does the author get all this information?
"Moving the magnet makes current flow in the wire."	
"The lightning hit a tree and knocked it down." →	Why does lightning always hit trees?
"During a lightning storm: go into a house, car, or bus." →	If a bus is made of metal, isn't it bad to go into a bus or car?

Student's Dialogue Journal

LEARNING LOGS

Learning log entries, unlike Journal entries, are centered around questions or writing frames, which can be provided to students by the teacher or chosen by the student from a menu. Below is a menu of forty writing frames, called CREATE IDEAS. These frames are based on eleven distinct types of thinking and can be rotated over the course of the year to develop students' capacities as writers and thinkers.

C	**Compare & Contrast**	*To determine differences or similarities on the basis of certain criteria:* • List similarities and differences. • Compare and contrast the following _____. • What are the significant similarities or differences between _____ and _____? • Which two are most similar or most different?
R	**Relate Personally**	*To describe one's emotional state or feeling or how one would apply what was learned to some part of his or her own life:* • What are your feelings about _____? • How would you feel if _____ happened to you? • What would you do if _____ happened to you? • What are some possible feelings you had when that happened?
E	**Evaluate**	*To appraise the value or worth of a thing or idea or to make a quantitative or qualitative judgment concerning specific criteria:* • Which alternative would you choose and why? • What are the advantages or disadvantages of _____? • Given the following choices, justify or substantiate your selection.
A	**Associate**	*To relate objects/thoughts as they come to mind:* • Free, controlled, or linked association. • What words/ideas come to mind when I say _____? • What do you think of when you listen to the _____? • What do you think of when you see the _____?
T	**Trace/ Sequence**	*To arrange information in a logical order according to chronology, quantity, quality, or location:* • Trace the development of _____. • Sequence the events leading up to _____. • What do you do first when you _____?
E	**Enumerate**	*To list in concise form or to name one after another:* • List the causes of the _____. • List the facts regarding _____. • List the steps involved in _____.

| **CREATE IDEAS writing frames**

Continued on the next page

I	**Identify & Describe**	*To identify the properties of particular items, happenings, or concepts:* • What did you see, hear, note? • Describe the facts. • What did you observe? • Describe the characteristics or properties of the object.
D	**Define**	*To give the meaning of a word or concept:* • Define the following concept. • Define what is meant by _____? • Define the word from the context clues.
E	**Explore & Predict**	*To generate alternatives and assumptions concerning cause and effect:* • How many ways can you _____? • What would happen if _____? • Suppose _____ happened? What would be the consequences?
A	**Argue a Position**	*To explain good reasons for a particular position; to present facts to support your position:* • Where do you stand on this issue? • Justify your position. • Explain your argument. • What are your reasons for taking this position?
S	**Summarize**	*To state briefly or in conclusive form the substance of what has been observed, heard, or experienced:* • Summarize what you read. • Think of a title for the story. • Draw a picture that summarizes what you learned. • The point of view of the lecture was _____.

In the following examples, two teachers explain their experience with Learning Logs and discuss sample student work.

Proficient Reader's Logs

Janet Barrilogna
Fourth-Grade Teacher

"I guess one of the most important experiences of my career was reading *The Mosaic of Thought* by Ellin Keene and Susan Zimmermann. Up until then I'd been using a sort of modified whole language approach. What that book did was show me how to organize it. I divide my year into eight units—two for each of the four proficient reader skills they discuss: metacognition, questioning, synthesizing, and imagery. Half of these units are in literature and half are nonfiction. Anyway, I start a unit by modeling the skill during mini-lessons. Then during readers' workshops, students use their learning logs to work with that skill on books they've chosen for themselves. Mark's entry comes from one of our units on imagery. Just look at that language!"

Mark Schweitzer
Fourth Grade

Learning Log Entry—Focus Skill: Imagery

I remember how it was on the trail. I could hear the wind blow. The squeaky wheels were loud too. The two oxen we had were big and brown. When it got really hot you could see sweat dripping down their faces.
    When we got to Oregon the wagon looked old. It turned gray from all the dust and dirt. The wagon was covered with mud and some of the wood was cracked. It looked like a different wagon than the wagon we left in.

| **Student's Learning Log**

Learning Log Menu Approach

Bill Paxson
Fifth-Grade Teacher

"I had to learn the hard way. My first year out I just gave the kids a menu of questions they could ask themselves about reading and asked them to read, pick a question, and answer it. Well, by the end of the first month I could see the results were terrible. The kids' responses were hopelessly vague and didn't answer the question. And they gravitated to the questions they felt were easiest. I saw an awful lot of drawings, not much writing. This was no good. So I backed up and started over. I'd select a kind of question—just one—for a week or two. I'd model it, ask the kids to focus on it, and read strong examples during sharing time. I built in a revision cycle too. I showed the kids how to select their best answer to one type of question and rework it to make it better. Not right away, but eventually I saw real improvement. It's hard, but you know what? Teaching reading and writing *is* rocket science. Just as hard, just as rewarding. Anyway, for this particular week, we were working on building arguments. I chose Miles's example because I liked how he stated his position up front and then used evidence from the reading to support it." (See diagram on next page.)

Miles Arnold   Fifth Grade

Learning Log Entry – Focus Skill: Argument

Martin Luther King Jr. was a great man. He was great because of his personality and belief in equality. He was also great because he lived at the right time.

There were people before Martin Luther King Jr. who wanted equality, but America wasn't ready to listen. Dr. King got his message across because America was ready to listen. Because of the war, the army was not segregated any more. Segregation was also made illegal in schools in 1954. So things were starting to change even before Dr. King.

Martin Luther King Jr. gave great speeches about equality and about how segregation was unjust. Americans could see the African American soldiers who fought for America treated poorly. The people were ready to listen.

In 1964 the Civil Rights Act was signed. This could not have happened without the strong beliefs of Dr. King. It also could not have happened if the country was not ready to listen to Dr. King.

Student's Learning Log

KINDLING

The Strategy in Action

Joanne Aliazar introduces her students to their Learning Logs (see page 131) by using a strategy known as Kindling.

Joanne: The books you have in front of you are very important. They are your Learning Logs. You are going to use your Learning Log all year long—to explore ideas, ask questions, and think about how what you're learning affects your life. It will become a record of you—of how you think and what you like and don't like. I want to begin today's lesson by showing you how Learning Logs work. And I'm going to start with a strange question: Does anyone know what kindling is?

Jack: Isn't that like tree branches?

Joanne: Yes, that's right. Does anyone know more about kindling?

Hayley: They're little branches.

Joanne: That's also correct. Does anyone know what kindling is used for?

Ellen: In the winter, my father lights fires in our basement. I help him. He carries in the big logs and I carry in the kindling branches.

Joanne: And what do you and your father do with the kindling?

Ellen: We put it at the bottom of the fire to make the big logs catch on fire.

Joanne: That's exactly right. Kindling is how you start a fire. A good fire begins with small dry branches that catch fire quickly and that help to ignite a larger flame. What we're going to learn today is how to kindle your thinking, how to make little ideas into big and powerful ones. Think back for a minute about what you learned yesterday during our computer lab and in our reading from *Computers for Kids*. Now think about this: only twenty years ago, almost no one owned or knew how to use a personal computer. Why do you think computers have become so important so quickly? Spend a minute or two thinking about this question. [Joanne pauses for two minutes while students write.] Next, I want you to pair up with a partner and share your ideas with each other. Together, note which ideas are similar and which are different. Then, as a team, generate one new idea about why computers became so popular. [Joanne pauses for three minutes while students work.] So what ideas did you come up with? [Joanne surveys student responses.]

Chuck: Computers help people because you can use them for writing papers. They have whole encyclopedias on CDs to help you get ideas for writing. And you use the word processor for typing it.

Jon: The Internet lets people talk to each other and find lots of information.

Ashley: My mother and I found out that computers aren't as expensive as she thought. So we bought one.

Caryn: They're fun to use. They use bright colors. And the music is neat too.

Maria: We have a program that helps me with my math homework.

Boris: My father uses a money program to help him keep track of our money.

Krystof: My brother just bought a new baseball bat on our computer.

[During this student response period, Joanne keeps track of student answers on the board by building a web.]

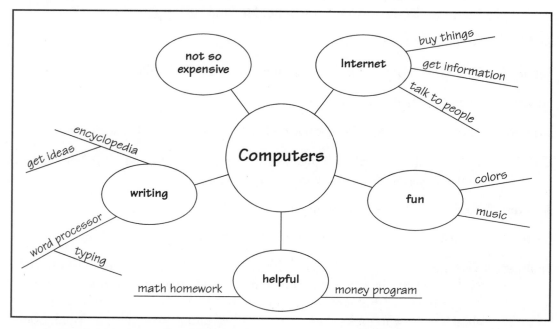

| *Web organizer for capturing information to use in a Learning Log activity*

Joanne: All your ideas are great. We now know that some of the reasons computers became so popular so quickly are that they're fun, they're helpful, they're good for writing, they're not so expensive to buy, and because the Internet lets you get information, buy things, and talk to people. Now, I want you to use the class's ideas to think some more about computers. Turn to page three in *Computers for Kids* and read the section entitled "Welcome to the Computer Age." Then meet with your partner to discuss the reading. Note which things in the reading are similar to the ideas we came up with and which are different. When you are finished, write a brief entry in your Learning Log that explains three ways the world has changed because of computers. Use the ideas from our discussion and those from the reading to create this entry.

Tin Nguyen, a second-grade teacher, also uses Kindling. To make his Kindling lessons especially focused, he uses a set of icons he has placed on flashcards to cue his students to engage in productive learning behaviors. These icons, which Tin models with students at the beginning of the year, appear below:

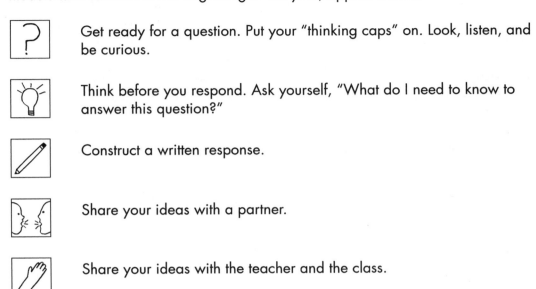

Get ready for a question. Put your "thinking caps" on. Look, listen, and be curious.

Think before you respond. Ask yourself, "What do I need to know to answer this question?"

Construct a written response.

Share your ideas with a partner.

Share your ideas with the teacher and the class.

Why the Strategy Is Beneficial

The model lesson you have just read employs the Kindling strategy (Silver, Strong, & Commander, 1998). At the literal level, Kindling is, as Joanne mentioned, a technique for starting a fire. A good fire begins with small pieces of dry wood that catch fire quickly and help to ignite a larger flame. The same is true for kindling a question: with the correct technique, we can ignite student thinking and student writing.

Kindling is a questioning technique used to create anticipation and promote involvement in new learning. It is used to enhance classroom participation, ensure class discussion, and deepen the connections between reading, thinking, and writing.

The strategy achieves these goals because:

- It provides students with significant time to construct a quality response before they answer the question, thereby eliminating impulsive answering and making covert thinking overt.
- It asks students to process information and create a quality response in four separate ways. First, students think about the question on their own. Then, they write their answers in their Learning Logs. Next, they discuss and refine their answers with a partner. Finally, students share and discuss their ideas with the whole class and the teacher.
- It builds security for students who are tentative about participating. Kindling ensures that all students think about the question, since every learner is required to generate a response on paper. The strategy also includes a sharing process, which allows students to test their ideas in small groups before sharing with the whole class.

Kindling questions can be used as hooks to connect with student's prior learning and experience. Kindling can also be used throughout the lesson either to generate thoughts or to check for understanding. Below are four examples of Kindling questions:

- Think for a moment about what you know about communities and about what people do in communities. Share your ideas with a neighbor. Note which ideas are the same and which are different.
- Imagine you came back to America 300 years from now and discovered it was no longer a great power. What do you suppose caused this change in power? Share your ideas with a neighbor and generate one new idea together.
- Here are two long-division problems. What difference do you note between the two? Jot down thoughts and ideas. Meet with a neighbor and compare your ideas. Explain how you would solve the problems.
- Think about a time when you were really scared. Share your ideas with a neighbor. How does your time of fear compare with Harriet Tubman's?

How to Use the Strategy

Incorporate the Kindling strategy into your classroom using the following steps:

1. After reading, pose an open-ended question for students to consider on their own.
2. Have students pause and think about what they need to know to answer the question.
3. Ask students to "jot down," write, or even sketch their responses in their Journals or Learning Logs.
4. After students have recorded their ideas, ask them to share their written thoughts with either a neighbor or a small group. The students can synthesize ideas, critique each other's responses, determine the similarities and difference in their responses, or generate additional ideas.
5. Survey student responses to determine how many students have similar ideas, and record the ideas on the board so that they can be examined and explored further.

HELPING THE STRUGGLING WRITER

In applying information to their reading lives, struggling readers face one large problem: elaboration. They are frequently unable to generate enough ideas to produce interesting and thoughtful entries. This dilemma results from one of three factors or a combination of these factors.

- **Memory:** Struggling readers simply may not remember a text well enough to write about it.
- **Connection to Prior Knowledge:** Struggling readers may remember and be able to retell a text, but the information in the text is isolated—disconnected from other knowledge and experience. This makes it extremely difficult to write meaningfully about text content.
- **Text Structure:** Since struggling readers rarely read very much on their own, they are unfamiliar with text structure. When asked to write about reading, therefore, they have a great deal of difficulty planning what to write because they cannot readily imagine what elements make up a thoughtful response to a writing prompt, let alone generate an open response of their own.

Some of the suggestions below may help alleviate these problems.

Memory of the Text: Since struggling readers frequently don't remember a text well enough to write about it, asking them to look back at the text and retell it or helping them to create a set of notes on the text may provide a sufficient platform on which they can build a more thoughtful response.

Connection to Prior Knowledge and Experience: Notice the problem is not that the student lacks the knowledge or experience. If that were the case, the only solution would be for the teacher to provide the relevant knowledge by telling the student what he needs to know or by providing background readings. The problem here is that the knowledge in the text has been separated, locked in a mental compartment away from the students' own knowledge and experience. Rebuilding the connection can be accomplished in a number of ways.

- Use the Mind's Eye strategy (Chapter Three). Ask the student to read over the passage and identify five or six key words and phrases. Then ask the student to close her eyes and create images connected to those words and phrases. Finally, help the student use these images to create a response.
- Use the Think Aloud strategy. Ask the student to read the passage aloud and stop whenever a thought occurs to her. Keep a running record of the student's thoughts as she reads. Then help her use these thoughts as a platform to build a response.

- Use Concept Maps (Chapter Two). Provide the student with a list of five to six key vocabulary elements from the reading. Ask the student to place the words or phrases in circles and draw lines outward from each. At the end of each line ask the student to record something he learned from the text that relates to the idea in each circle. Now ask the student to add two or three more lines to each circle and help him to generate ideas, experiences, thoughts, or feelings related to each.

Understanding of Text Structure: This difficulty is not with the structure of the text the student has read, but the structure of the text she wants to produce. In this case, the student may face one of two problems. If the informal writing is an open response, the student's own thoughts may be too confused to permit her to get started. On the other hand, if the informal writing expected of her is a response to a question ("Compare animals in a desert community with animals that live in your neighborhood"), the lack of understanding of text structure may make it very difficult for her to generate an answer. In both cases, the problem is primarily organizational. Since teachers often encourage spontaneous writing in Journals and Learning Logs, they frequently take a hands-off policy when students write informally, but this approach misses the extreme difficulties some struggling readers face in being spontaneous. Their organizational disabilities in effect block their ability to be spontaneous in a meaningful way. In response to this situation a teacher can:

- Provide a generalization a student can use to get her writing started (e.g., "I think desert animals lead a much harder life than the animals in my neighborhood").
- Provide students with an appropriate graphic organizer to group and reshape their thoughts (Chapter One).
- Use the Inductive Learning strategy (Chapter Three). Ask the student to generate a list of things she might want to say. Then help her group and label them by common characteristics.

ASSESSMENT OPPORTUNITIES FOR WRITING FROM READING

In thinking about assessment, a clear distinction needs to be made: Do we want our assessments to be more like a window or more like a ruler?

A common misconception about assessment concerns its purpose. Most people assume that the purpose of assessment is evaluation of student progress. In this view we observe students, confer with them, and examine their work in order to measure their progress on a scale of achievement. But this ruler-like vision of assessment is only half the story. We can also use assessment to gain insights into students' interests, concerns, preoccupations, and styles of thinking. Assessment should serve as a window into how students work and think as well as a ruler for measuring their progress.

Assessment as a Window

Perhaps no strategies we have studied provide better windows into student thinking than those associated with informal writing. For example, one student writes:

> The story of Rosa Parks is incredible. She's like a real hero. She started something so big. So important. And just by doing something really simple. I want to learn more about Rosa Parks.
>
> I want to know what she's doing now. I want to know what she would say to me about things in my life. Like what do you do to be so strong?

Another student declares:

> Sometimes people can change the world. Rosa Parks is like this. People in her time were very prejudiced against certain people, especially African Americans. But people should not be prejudiced against anyone and Rosa Parks believed in equality. So she did something about it. I admire Rosa Parks because she saw what needed to happen and she made it happen. Now the world is not as prejudiced as it used to be.

In these examples, we can see much more than how well students are doing. We can see their interests, their concerns, and their personal styles of reading and thinking. Teachers need to keep records not only of students' progress but of the other aspects they learn about students through observation, discussion, and examination of student writing—both formal and informal. One way to address this issue is to keep a running record of what you learn about students' reading and learning. Look, for instance, at the following Weekly Reading Record kept by the teacher of these two students.

Weekly Reading Record				
	Reading	**Interests**	**Thinking**	**Next Steps**
Morris	Biography of Rosa Parks	Seems very engaged in our biography study. Possible connection to hero study last month.	Imaginative. Likes to ask "What if?" Interested in relationship between himself and Rosa Parks.	Writes sparsely—big ideas, not so many details. Reads for a little while then dreams. Try visual organizers to focus.
Wende	Biography of Rosa Parks	Interested in history and idea of change	Organized—likes to argue. Likes to find cause and effects. Likes Rosa Parks because she takes action.	Give her *Nettie's Trip South*. Ask which is better history: biography or historical fiction.

Students' reading experience recorded, and teacher's next step devised

Assessment as a Ruler

Looked at from a more ruler-like, evaluative perspective, informal writing, whether in Journals or Learning Logs, resembles a portfolio. In both cases we have a collection of pieces arranged over time. This directs our attention not at the single piece but at student progress across an array of pieces. This change in orientation—looking at many pieces rather than just one—changes the nature of the questions we ask about student work. In looking at students' informal writing this way, we ask ourselves:

- Is the student making progress in her ability to generate thoughtful responses that go beyond the information given? (Insight)
- In which kinds of writing (process entries, comparisons, personal responses, reviews, or critiques) is the student making the most progress? Which kinds of writing is she avoiding or writing in only a minimal way? (Flexibility)

- Overall, is the student's ability to build on her ideas (to use examples and evidence and to consider other points of view) increasing? (Development)
- Where is the student around richness of language and variety of sentence structure now as opposed to last month? (Language)
- How about writing conventions? What kinds of spelling and punctuation errors has she mastered? What conventions still elude her? (Conventions)
- On the whole, what is the level of organization that marks this student's writing? Is her spontaneous writing more organized and easier to follow than it was in September? (Organization)

Viewed in this light, a teacher might keep a different sort of running record of her learnings about her students reading as revealed in their informal writing.

Weekly Reading Record					
Morris — November					
Insight	**Organization**	**Development**	**Flexibility**	**Conventions**	**Language**
1 2 ③ 4	1 ② 3 4	1 ② 3 4	1 2 ③ 4	1 2 ③ 4	1 2 3 ④
Good ideas. Need more of them.	Doesn't write much—hard to tell.	Here's where we need work.	Fine.	Great with familiar word spellings. Now get him to look up the unfamiliar.	Wonderful. Introduce him to dialogue.

Reading record showing student's progress and where student needs help

Bibliography

Afflerbach, P.P., & Johnson, P.H. (1986). What do expert readers do when the main idea is not explicit? In J.F. Baumann (Ed.), *Teaching main idea comprehension* (49–72). Newark, DE: International Reading Association.

Anderson, R.C., & Pearson, P.D. (1984). A schema-theoretic view of basic processes in reading comprehension. In P.D. Pearson (Ed.) *Handbook of reading research.* New York: Longman.

Baumann, J.F., & Serra, J.K. (1984). The frequency and placement of main ideas in children's social studies textbooks. *Journal of Reading Behavior, 16,* 27–40.

Beck, I.L., McKeown, M.G., & Gromroll, E.W. (1989). Learning from social studies texts. *Cognition and Instruction, 6,* 99–158.

Beck, I.L., McKeown, M.G., Hamilton, R.L., & Kucan, L. (1997). *Questioning the author: An approach for enhancing student engagement with text.* Newark, DE: International Reading Association.

Brown, H., & Cambourne, B. (1987). *Read and retell.* Portsmouth, NH: Heinemann.

Brownlie, F., Close, S., & Wingren, L. (1990). *Tomorrow's classrooms today: Strategies for creating active readers, writers, and thinkers.* Markham, Ontario: Pembroke Publishers, Ltd.

Bruner, J. (1986). *Actual minds, possible worlds.* Cambridge, MA: Harvard University Press.

Burns, P.C., Roe, B.D., & Ross, E.P. (1998). *Teaching reading in today's elementary schools* (7th ed.). Boston: Houghton Mifflin.

Butler, K. (1984). *Learning and teaching style in theory and practice.* Columbia, CT: The Learner's Dimension.

Cole, J., & Degen, B. (1997). *The magic school bus and the electric field trip.* New York: Scholastic Press.

Collier, J.L., & Collier, C. (1989). *My brother Sam is dead.* New York: Scholastic Paperbacks.

Cunningham, J.W., & Moore, D.W. (1986). The confused world of main idea. In J.F. Baumann (Ed.), *Teaching main idea comprehension* (1–17). Newark, DE: International Reading Association.

Derewianka, B. (1990). *Exploring how texts work.* Newtown, Australia: Primary English Teaching Association.

Doctorow, M., Wittrock, M.C., & Marks, C. (1978). Generative processes in reading comprehension. *Journal of Educational Psychology, 70,* 109–118.

Escondido School District (1979). *Mind's Eye.* Escondido, CA: Board of Education.

Fisher, B. (1995). Things take off: Note taking in the first grade. In P. Cordeiro (Ed.), *Endless possibilities: Generating curriculum in social studies and literacy (21–32).* Portsmouth, NH: Heinemann.

Gambrell, L.B., & Bales, R.J. (1986). Mental imagery and the comprehension-monitoring performance of fourth- and fifth-grade poor readers. *Reading Research Quarterly, 21,* 454–464.

Hanson, J.R., Dewing, T., Silver, H.F., & Strong, R.W. (1991). Within our reach: Identifying and working more effectively with at-risk learners. *Students At-Risk* (Produced for the 1991 ASCD Conference, San Francisco, CA). Alexandria, VA: Association for Supervision and Curriculum Development.

Heller, R. (1983). *The reasons for a flower.* Fort Worth, TX: Alice Craighead Books.

Herber, H. (1970). *Teaching reading in the content areas.* Englewood Cliffs, NJ: Prentice Hall.

Herrman, B.A. (1992). Teaching and assessing strategic reasoning: Dealing with the dilemmas. *Reading Teacher, 45*(6), 428–433.

Hornblow, L., & Hornblow, A. (1970). *Reptiles do the strangest things.* New York: Random House.

Jones, B.F., Pierce, J., & Hunter, B. (1988–89). Teaching students to construct graphic representations. *Educational Leadership, 46*(4), 20–25.

Jung, C. (1923). *Psychological types* (transl. H.G. Baynes). New York: Harcourt, Brace & Co.

Just, M.A., & Carpenter, P.A. (1987). *The psychology of reading and language comprehension.* Rockleigh, NJ: Allyn & Bacon.

Kalbag, A. (1997). *World wide web for beginners.* Tulsa, OK: EDC Publishing.

Keene, E.O., & Zimmermann, S. (1997). *Mosaic of thought: Teaching comprehension in a reader's workshop.* Portsmouth, NH: Heinemann.

Kosovo's Sorrow. (1999). *Time for Kids,* 4(23), 4–5.

Lawrence, J. (1993). *Harriet and the promised land.* New York: Simon and Schuster Books for Young Readers.

Lehman, H.G. (1992). Graphic organizers benefit slow learners. *The Clearing House, 66*(1), 53–55.

Leon, V. (1998). *Outrageous women of the middle ages.* New York: John Wiley and Sons.

Lyman, F. (Compiler), & American Museum of Natural History. (1998). *Inside the Dzanga Sangha rainforest: Exploring the heart of central Africa.* New York: Workman Publishing Co.

Marzano, R.J. (1992). *A different kind of classroom: Teaching with dimensions of learning.* Alexandria, VA: Association for Supervision and Curriculum Development.

Marzano, R.J., & Paynter, D.E. (1994). *New approaches to literacy: Helping students develop reading and writing skills.* Washington, D.C.: American Psychological Association.

McCarthy, B. (1982). *The 4Mat system.* Arlington Heights, IL: Excel Publishing Co.

Miller, W. (1997). *Richard Wright and the library card.* New York: Lee & Low Books.

Moore, D.W., Cunningham, J.W., & Rudisill, N.J. Readers' conception of the main idea. In J.A. Niles and L.A. Harris (Eds.), *Searching for meaning in reading/language processing and instruction.* Thirty-second yearbook of the National Reading Conference (pp.202–206). Chicago: National Reading Conference.

Moore, D.W., Readence, J.E., & Rickelman, R.J. (1989). *Prereading activities for content area reading and learning.* Newark, DE: International Reading Association.

Morrow, L.M. (1983). Reading and retelling stories: Strategies for emergent readers. *The Reading Teacher, 38,* 870–875.

Moses, L.J. (1997). *The most amazing treehouse ever.* Woodbridge, NJ: Thoughtful Education Press.

Mullis, I.V.S., Owen, G.H., & Phillips, G.W. (1990). *America's challenge: Accelerating academic achievement (a summary of findings from 20 years of NAEP).* Princeton, NJ: Educational Testing Service.

Muth, D.K. (1987). Structure strategies for comprehending expository text. *Reading Research and Instruction, 27*(1), 66–72.

Myers, I.B. (1962). *The Myers-Briggs type indicator.* Palo Alto, CA: Consulting Psychologists Press.

Ogle, D. (1986). K-W-L: A teaching model that develops active reading of the expository text. *The Reading Teacher, 39,* 564–570.

Pauk, W. (1974). *How to study in college.* Boston: Houghton Mifflin.

Pearson, P.D., & Comperell, K. (1994). Comprehension of Text Structures. In R.B. Ruddell, H. Singer, & M.R. Ruddell (Eds.), *Theoretical Models and Processes of Reading* (4th ed.), (pp.448–468). Newark, DE: International Reading Association.

Pearson, P.D., & Johnson, D.D. (1978). *Teaching reading comprehension.* New York: Holt, Rinehart, & Winston.

Perfetti, C.A. (1985). *Reading ability.* New York: Oxford University Press.

Pressley, M. (1976). Mental imagery helps eight-year-olds remember what they read. *Journal of Educational Psychology, 68,* 355–359.

Pressley, M. (1977). Imagery and children's learning: Putting the picture in developmental perspective. *Review of Educational Research, 47,* 586–622.

Raphael, T.E. (1982). Question-answering strategies for children. *The Reading Teacher. 36:* 186–190.

Raphael, T.E., & McKinney, J. (1983). An examination of fifth and eighth grade students' question answering behavior: An instructional study in metacognition. *Journal of Reading Behavior, 15,* 67–86.

Raphael, T.E., & Pearson, P.D. (1982). *The effect of metacognitive awareness training on children's question-answering behavior* (Tech. Rep. No.238). Urbana: University of Illinois, Center for the Study of Reading.

Raphael, T.E., Wonnacott, C.A., & Pearson, P.D. (1983). *Increasing students' sensitivity to sources of information: An instructional study in question-answer relationships* (Tech. Rep. No.284). Urbana: University of Illinois, Center for the Study of Reading.

Richardson, J.S., & Morgan, R.F. (1997). *Reading to learn in the content areas.* (3rd edition). New York: Wadsworth Publishing.

Robinson, A. (1997). *Sam's soccer problem.* Woodbridge, NJ: Thoughtful Education Press.

Robinson, A., & Moses, L.J. (1997). *Bobby's biking lesson.* Woodbridge, NJ: Thoughtful Education Press.

Ruta, K.W. (1992). Teaching text patterns to remedial readers. *Journal of Reading, 35,* 657–658.

Sadoski, M. (1985). The natural use of imagery in story comprehension and recall: Replication and extension. *Reading Research Quarterly, 19,* 110–123.

Saffer, B. (1998). Danger from the sky. *Cricket Magazine,* Oct., 21–26.

Santa, C.M., Havens, L.T., & Maycumber, E.M. (1996). *Project CRISS: Creating independence through student-owned strategies* (2nd Edition). Dubuque, IA: Kendall/Hunt.

Sharmat, M. (1983). *Gregory the terrible eater.* New York: Scholastic Press.

Siegel, M.G. (1984). *Reading as signification.* Doctoral dissertation, Indiana University, Bloomington.

Silver, H.F., & Hanson, J.R. (1991). *Hanson Silver learning preference inventory.* Woodbridge, NJ: Thoughtful Education Press.

Silver, H.F., & Hanson, J.R. (1998). *Learning styles and strategies* (3rd edition). Woodbridge, NJ: Thoughtful Education Press.

Silver, H.F., Hanson, J.R., Strong, R.W., & Schwartz, P.B. (1996). *Teaching styles and strategies* (3rd edition). Trenton, NJ: Thoughtful Education Press.

Silver, H.F., & Strong, R.W. (1994). *Reading styles and strategies.* Trenton, NJ: Thoughtful Education Press.

Silver, H.F., Strong, R.W., & Commander, J. (1998). *Tools for promoting active, in-depth learning.* Woodbridge, NJ: Thoughtful Education Press.

Silver, H.F., Strong, R.W., & Perini, M.P. (in press). *Tools II: More techniques for promoting active, in-depth learning.* Trenton, NJ: Thoughtful Education Press.

Sparks, J.E. (1982). *Write for power.* Los Angeles: Communication Associates.

Strong, R.W., Hanson, J.R., & Silver, H.F. (1995). *Questioning styles and strategies* (2nd edition). Woodbridge, NJ: Thoughtful Education Press.

Taba, H. (1971). *Hilda Taba teaching strategies program.* Miami, FL: Institute for Staff Development.

Taylor, B.M., & Beach, R.W. (1984). The effects of text structure instruction on middle grade students' comprehension and production of expository text. *Reading Research Quarterly, 19,* 134–146.

Thomas, E. (1998). *Styles and strategies for teaching middle grades mathematics.* Woodbridge, NJ: Thoughtful Education Press.

Tierney, R.J., & Cunningham, P.M. (1984). Research on teaching reading comprehension. In P.D. Pearson (Ed.), Handbook of reading research. New York: Longman.

Turner, R.M. (1991). *Georgia O'Keefe.* New York: Little, Brown & Co.

Vacca, R.T., & Vacca, J.L. (1998). *Content area reading: Literacy and learning across the curriculum.* New York: Longman.

van Dijk, T.A., & Kintsch, W. (1983). *Strategies of discourse comprehension.* New York: Academic Press.

White, J.B. (1984). *When words lose their meaning: Constitutions and reconstitutions of language, character, and community.* Chicago: The University of Chicago Press.

Other Books by Silver Strong & Associates

Available from Canter & Associates, the publisher of *Discovering Nonfiction*

Learning Styles and Strategies
The most in-depth and practical introduction to the different ways students learn. Discover how to address the diversity of learning styles in your classroom and how to develop style-based curriculum, instruction, and assessment practices.

Teaching Styles and Strategies
Twenty-five research-based instructional strategies that develop students' skills in:

- Organizing and mastering information.
- Understanding and critical thinking.
- Self-expression and creativity.
- Interpersonal and cooperative learning.

Questioning Styles and Strategies
More than thirty questioning strategies designed to actively engage students' minds and encourage them to think in a variety of ways.

The Learning Preference Inventory
Based on Carl Jung's renowned theory of personality type, the Learning Preference Inventory is the most valid and reliable tool for finding out which learning activities and teaching methods motivate each of your students, including at-risk and gifted learners.

To order and to request a free catalog, call Canter & Associates at 800-262-4347.

More Books by Silver Strong & Associates

Tools for Promoting Active, In-Depth Learning
Sixty classroom-tested, ready-to-use techniques for actively engaging students in meaningful learning.

You've Got Style!
A series of story and activity books that are a fun and effective way to teach learning styles to primary students.

- Bobby's Biking Lesson
- Sam's Soccer Problem
- The Most Amazing Treehouse Ever

Thinkers' Guides to Literature and Social Studies
Curriculum units based on extensive research into the skills most commonly tested in the new state assessments. These guides combine the insights of learning styles, multiple intelligences, and teaching strategies into an easy-to-use format.

- **Literature:** The Giver, My Brother Sam Is Dead, In the Year of the Boar and Jackie Robinson, The Pushcart War, The Drinking Gourd, Bridge to Terabithia
- **Social Studies:** A Thinker's Guide to Ancient Egypt, A Thinker's Guide to the Age of Explorers

To order and to request a free catalog, call Silver Strong & Associates at 800-962-4432, or order online at *www.silverstrong.com*.

Graduate-Level Video Course

Teaching Reading in the Elementary Grades
Help students thrive as independent readers. Learn research-based strategies to increase students' vocabulary, enhance fluency, and build comprehension.

Building Your Repertoire of Teaching Strategies
Learn advanced teaching strategies to achieve your learning objectives. See immediate results as more of your students respond as learners and thinkers.

For more information about this course and other graduate-level courses, contact Canter & Associates at 800-669-9011, or visit *www.canter.net*.